No. 8 in the Harnessing Health Information series

Series Editor
Michael Rigby

Harnessing Information for Health Economics Analysis

Marilyn James

Senior Lecturer in Health Economics
Centre for Health Planning and Management, Keele University

and

Elizabeth Stokes

Research Assistant in Health Services Research
Centre for Health Planning and Management, Keele University

Radcliffe Publishing
Oxford · Seattle

Radcliffe Publishing Ltd
18 Marcham Road
Abingdon
Oxon OX14 1AA
United Kingdom

www.radcliffe-oxford.com
Electronic catalogue and worldwide online ordering facility.

British Library Cataloguing in Publication Data

A catalogue record for this book is available from the British Library.

ISBN-10 1 85775 985 0
ISBN-13 978 1 85775 985 3

Typeset by Anne Joshua & Associates, Oxford
Printed and bound by TJ International Ltd, Padstow, Cornwall

Contents

Series editor's preface

This latest volume in the *Harnessing Health Information* series marks a timely step forward. Health economic evaluation is an important applied technique for decision makers. Faced with difficult decisions on service provision choices, investment alternatives, and deployment of existing resources, as well as new diagnostic and treatment techniques, managers and clinicians need a sound basis for rational selection. This is provided by health economics methods.

The frequent misunderstanding is that these methods are based solely on financial costs. Instead, a fundamental feature of health economics analyses is to assess and quantify the overall gain (or loss) in terms of benefits and costs between alternatives. Health economic analysis measures value, not price, and thus can be applied to any assessment or evaluation.

The main challenge is in finding the data to drive effective and relevant analyses. Special data collection is an expensive exercise and should not be undertaken lightly; meanwhile the NHS, and other health partners, are custodians of large amounts of data that are not fully exploited. Therefore the highly topical task of the authors of this text is to signpost the data sources and information available to those undertaking health economic studies.

Marilyn James and Elizabeth Stokes bring significant practical expertise to bear. Both are experienced in running applied studies, from large-scale pharmaceutical and other treatment technology studies, to locally commissioned NHS assessments. They thus each bring academic rigour and sound technical knowledge sharpened by considerable operational experience. This is not a book about health economics methodologies, but about how to fuel and run those methodologies with sound information, without which they are impracticable concepts.

Information and its use are in general under-valued in the NHS. This book will enable existing data to be put to good use, and better decisions to be made based on sound evaluations of impact as much as cost. It focuses on a very important and valuable setting for *Harnessing Health Information.*

Michael Rigby
March 2006

About the authors

Dr Marilyn James BA (Hons) MSc PhD is a Senior Lecturer in Health Economics and founding head of the Health Economics (R&D) Unit at the Centre for Health Planning and Management, Keele University, since 1995. She graduated in economics at Liverpool University in 1987, after which she completed an MSc in health economics at York University. In 1993 she gained a doctorate from the University of Manchester. She is economic advisor to the Department of Health's National Screening Committee Antenatal Sub Group.

After completing her MSc, Marilyn gained practical knowledge of the health service by working in a variety of posts both at district and unit level across the NHS. During her doctoral studies she was employed as the health economist to West Lancashire Health Authority. Before taking up post in the Centre in January 1994, she worked for the Department of Medicines Management at Keele. Between 2001 and 2004 she gained commercial experience while on secondment to AstraZeneca pharmaceuticals, working as senior global health economist. She worked on mega-brand drugs and the design and delivery of major international trials, taking Crestor through the reimbursement process with a number of Prescription Pricing Authorities.

She has for many years provided technical and policy advice to regional NHS R&D directorates in the field of health economics. Marilyn's primary objective for her research is applied economic evaluation. Her current research portfolio is wide and is concentrated upon the practical application of economic evaluation in a number of research settings. These include evaluation in pharmaceuticals, nutritional support, orthopaedics, orthotics, ophthalmology (where she has been involved in preparing part of the National Service Framework in screening for diabetic eye disease), A&E (accident and emergency) medicine, obstetrics and gynaecology. In addition, she has applied cost utility analysis using both the Rosser QALY and the EuroQol indices to assist purchasers in making prioritisation decisions. Research funding has been obtained from the Department of Health, research councils, charities, regional health authorities, district health authorities through to individual practitioners. She has published and presented widely in the field of clinical and economic evaluation and applying health economics to policy issues.

Elizabeth Stokes BSc is a Research Assistant in Health Services Research at the Centre for Health Planning and Management, Keele University. She graduated in mathematics from Durham University in 1999. She is involved in a broad range of health services research with particular interests in health economics and medical statistics.

Elizabeth's time is spent on the conduct and management of a portfolio of externally funded research projects. She specialises in providing quantitative research support to projects from their research design to their analysis and final completion. She also has experience of qualitative techniques, including surveys and interviewing. Since 2001, she has been involved in many applied economic evaluations, and in particular in identifying and obtaining appropriate sources of data and information from primary and secondary sources. Elizabeth's areas of expertise include the management and analysis of data, and ensuring it is collected in a useable format.

Elizabeth has worked on projects funded by primary care trusts, regional health authorities, and biotechnology and pharmaceutical companies. She has been involved in several economic evaluations in nutritional support, both oral supplementation and enteral feeding, and musculoskeletal conditions such as neck disorders and shoulder pain. Elizabeth has been involved in dental services research projects including a workforce devlopment study in primary care. She is a grant holder for a service development study to evaluate patterns and quality of referrals for minor oral surgery from primary to secondary care. She has published economic evaluations and broader health service research papers from these studies.

1 Introduction and key concepts in health economics

Introduction

Healthcare and the delivery and consumption of such care are an interesting series of complex processes. The process of care includes diagnosis, treatment, prevention, rehabilitation and palliative care. Many individuals deliver this care within organisations ranging from the general practitioner (GP) or hospital trust to commercial organisations such as pharmaceutical companies and government bodies. At the same time resources available for healthcare remain scarce, while the demand for healthcare rises with new and competing treatments and an aging population. With finite resources difficult choices will always have to be made regarding the delivery and receipt of healthcare.

Given the demands made upon the healthcare system the allocation and evaluation of care must become an increasingly scientific process, no longer dependent solely on a first-come, first-served basis. It necessitates a clearer understanding of the costs and benefits of delivering and providing such care. Health economics and the tools and thought processes it utilises can help those concerned with the delivery and receipt of healthcare to make these decisions. It is from the discipline and perspective of health economics that this book is written, with a particular focus on the information which is necessary and available to support evaluation processes.

Scarcity

In a cash-limited healthcare environment, healthcare will always entail choices between goods and services. Demand for healthcare will exceed supply, and choices between competing goods and services will have to be made. This is the concept of scarcity; all demand cannot be satisfied with the existing level of resources. Choices as to which healthcare will be delivered and how much of the competing alternatives will be provided will have to be made.

Health economics is a tool to help decision makers make those choices in a rational fashion.

What is health economics?

Health economics measures the costs and benefits associated with healthcare. A number of different perspectives may be adopted from which to define the broad range of costs and benefits. These include a wide societal perspective, a narrower range of costs and benefits (for example, from the hospital's perspective), or the costs and benefits as they accrue to the recipient of care (the patient).

Health economics as a discipline seeks to achieve efficiency in terms of the competing healthcare options. It seeks to indicate the treatment or procedure that maximises benefits in respect to cost, or minimises cost with respect to benefit in terms of the competing options. This may be either within a single healthcare area, for example cholesterol-lowering drugs, or across healthcare areas, for example between orthopaedics and paediatric care. Health economics is concerned with all the costs and benefits of a good or service, not merely the financial costs or pecuniary benefits.

This book is primarily concerned with providing the reader with the tools to achieve the allocation of goods and services on efficiency grounds. Although equity issues and the allocation of goods and services on the grounds of equity – that is, the 'fair' distribution of goods and services – are important, they are not the primary focus of this book.

The difference between health and healthcare

Before proceeding further with the chapter it is necessary to clarify the distinction between health and healthcare. When an individual takes a tablet it is not because they gain satisfaction from taking the tablet, but rather because they believe that taking the tablet will serve to improve their general state of health. The demand for healthcare is, thus, a derived demand. Health *per se* cannot be purchased or traded but the commodity healthcare – whether it is in the form of a tablet, surgery or palliative care – can be traded and purchased between individuals. This chapter will focus upon the demand and supply of healthcare in terms of the benefits and costs it yields for individuals' and populations' health.

Terminology

It is important as a preparatory step to become familiar with some of the terminology and language of health economics. The tools of economic evaluation will be discussed in Chapter 2. Many terms used in everyday language have different or very specific meanings in health economics.

The following are some key terms in health economics.

Benefit

Benefit is the output of a healthcare process. It is the outcome of treatment or care. Benefit can encompass many different facets: it can be as simple as a positive or negative test result; a measurement of pain or mobility; or can encompass the much broader area of changes in quality of life. Benefit is largely thought of as the improvement to a patient's health status following an intervention; it can however encompass maintenance of health in the case of preventative, rehabilitative or palliative care. Benefit will be discussed more fully in Chapter 7.

Resources and cost

Resources represent the input into a healthcare intervention. In economics, resources are reported in natural units. It is to these natural units that monetary costs are then attached. A natural unit is the resource or event itself – for example, the bed day – rather than the cost attached to the bed day. Reporting in natural units rather than costs alone allows the findings of any work to be transferred across settings. By clearly specifying the natural unit rather than the cost, the information can be applied to the decision maker's own environment and local costs substituted for the ones reported. Costs are the monetary value of producing the resources. Sometimes prices rather than costs are reported. The price may be greater than the cost and represent an economic rent or profit over and above the actual cost for the producer.

It is the interaction between cost and benefit that is important in terms of economics. Chapter 2 will look specifically at the types of analysis to combine measures of cost and benefit. The relationship between the costs and the benefits defines whether an intervention is economically efficient or not.

Efficiency

In health economics it is the relationship between costs and benefits that is important, not merely the costs and benefits singularly. In order to achieve the efficient allocation of goods and services it is important therefore to:

- maximise benefit with respect to cost or
- minimise cost with respect to benefit.

Choice of care for treatments x and y could be represented in the following way, where treatment x is more efficient in terms of the benefits (B) with respect to costs (C) that it generates over treatment y:

$$\Sigma C_y / \Sigma B_y > \Sigma C_x / \Sigma B_x$$

Hence treatment x generates more benefits at less cost.

It is also important to highlight the distinction between technical efficiency and allocative efficiency.

Technical efficiency

Technical efficiency refers to choices made within goods and services. It is defined as:

- maximising benefit with respect to cost or
- minimising cost with respect to benefit in a single product.

This may include choices between the type of hip prosthesis, for example, or the delivery of surgical care such as open versus closed laparoscopy.

Allocative efficiency

In contrast allocative efficiency refers to choices made between goods and services. It is defined as:

- maximising benefit with respect to cost or
- minimising cost with respect to benefit across a range of goods or services.

This may include choices regarding allocation between prevention versus treatment (for example, cholesterol-lowering drugs versus cardiac care) or in providing funding across specialties, for example, for orthopaedics versus ophthalmology.

To compare goods and thus achieve efficiency a key requirement is that costs and benefits can be measured in common units across goods and services.

Opportunity cost

The opportunity cost is the value of a good in its next best alternative. Hence the opportunity cost is the benefits gained by one option expressed in terms of the benefits forgone by not doing the competing alternative.

The concept of value is an important issue here: value may often be thought of as being expressed in terms of a common monetary unit. By choosing to purchase a certain number of cataract operations at a given cost that provide a given benefit, there will be a specific number of hip replacements that could have been purchased to achieve the same level of cost or benefit. Hence the opportunity cost of the cataract replacements may be expressed in terms of the hip replacements forgone.

The concept is however more meaningful than this and should not merely reflect the monetary value placed upon a good or service, but in addition reflect the marginal utility or personal or collective benefit to be gained from a good or service. One may be prepared to sacrifice two bottles of cheaper wine to purchase one really good bottle, but may not be prepared to give up three bottles of cheaper wine to purchase one good bottle. Again in terms of economics it is about comparing the costs and benefits of one alternative good or service, or bundle of goods and services, over another competing alternative.

Scope of this book

This book is not a theoretical textbook, but an applied book designed to equip its readers with the practical tools to both understand and apply health economic methods. This book seeks to provide anyone faced with making choices, personal or interpersonal, regarding the supply or receipt of healthcare with the information to make informed decisions about that healthcare. It seeks to introduce the reader to the key economic tools and the data available that can assist an economic decision and how to use and interpret such data. Its aim is not to turn the decision maker into a health economist but to provide them with the ability to ask the appropriate questions, understand the relevant data and literature and to access the resources available to them.

Chapter 2 describes the key steps necessary for undertaking and understanding economic evaluation. The situations where such analysis would be useful are detailed. It introduces the reader to some of the key analytical methods for undertaking such analysis. This is considered alongside the checklist for good practice guidelines in economic appraisal.

Data are required in many different healthcare settings and at many different levels for economic decision making. At the macro level these are country-wide or national data. National data must both be fuelled and fed back into micro-economic data, at the level of the hospital trust and into primary care.

Considerable advances have been made in the provision of national cost data both at the level of the trust and at the national level, with data such as Healthcare Resource Groups (HRGs) and the National Schedule of Reference Costs.[1] These are data reported at the national level, but crucially based on improvements in the collection of secondary care data. Similarly data are available for primary care in the *Unit Costs of Health and Social Care*.[2] In terms of drug costs national data are available from sources such as the British National Formulary (BNF).[3] The cost data are supplemented by national outcomes statistics in areas such as cancer registers, mortality statistics and census data. The data which are available at the national, secondary care and primary care levels are discussed in Chapters 3, 4 and 5. Further, what is important for any healthcare analyst is the relationship and overlap at both the macro and micro levels in terms of the data available and uses in terms of health economics.

Many different organisations are responsible for providing health economic information. It is important to know what information is available that is of use to the economic analyst. A starting point may therefore be to consider key organisations responsible for data production, then look more closely at the type and uses of the information that they provide. The Department of Health (DH) is of course a key source of such data and provides the umbrella organisation for bodies such as the National Institute for Health and Clinical Excellence (NICE) and information such as technology appraisals. Other organisations may be publicly based (for example, bodies such as the Cochrane Collaboration) or privately funded (such as the Office of Health Economics). Chapter 6 looks both at the organisations providing health economic information and the type of information that they provide.

The measurement of benefits and resources or costs are the two mainstays of economics and the reasons for undertaking economic appraisal. Both concepts and their measurements are discussed in detail in Chapters 7 and 8 respectively. In Chapter 7 the concept of benefit as it applies to health economics is revisited, and examples of instruments for assessing benefits are considered and their appropriateness for different types of economic evaluation. Differences between generic and specific instruments are discussed. The chapter moves on to examine the concept of utility measurement and utility-based measures and their use in economic evaluation. The chapter concludes by examining some of the techniques for obtaining preference-based measures for health benefits or outcomes.

Chapter 8 revisits the definition of natural units and their importance in economic analysis. It looks at the advantages and disadvantages of collecting one's own data on resources or using pre-existing datasets. It suggests which types of resource or cost data the reader may wish to collect and distinguishes between the different types of costs – capital, staff, consumables, and direct and indirect costs – and suggests ways that such data may be collected in practice. Finally, it concludes by comparing the pros and cons of collecting data prospectively or retrospectively.

Coverage

This book will be particularly useful to those wishing to use and understand health economic information in a UK setting. In particular Chapters 3, 4 and 5 specifically discuss data available and applicable to the UK. Chapter 6 contains details both on UK and global information and organisations. Chapters 2, 7 and 8 focus on concepts that are universal in health economics, regardless of the country of origin.

The book covers a wide variety of information from broad aggregate national data down to designing and undertaking your own economic analysis. It covers a range of areas from primary care to national data to global indicators of health. It is designed to be helpful whether you are reading it with a view to designing national policy at a macro-economic level, or choosing the 'best' cardiovascular drug for your patient at a micro-economic level.

Users

Many participants in the healthcare arena will need to know about and understand health economic information, its availability and uses. This book will appeal to a number of potential users of health economic information. It will be especially useful in terms of the information and tools it presents for anyone who is involved in decision making in healthcare, whether policy maker, manager, clinician, therapist, nurse, scientist or researcher.

This book will guide the reader to information to help them make those decisions and introduce and explain the tools that they can use to undertake the choices.

Some readers of this book may be new to the discipline of health economics. They may have undertaken formal training in health economics, but may still be unclear from where information to undertake an economic evaluation is available and the level and type of information available. Conversely readers may be aware of the nature and extent of information available, but be unclear how best to utilise this information to assist in achieving a health economic solution to some of the day-to-day issues that they are facing. It is intended that this book will help the reader tackle such problems.

The rest of this book will guide the reader through each of the areas in turn. Although following a logical order throughout the book, each chapter will be self-contained in its own right, enabling the reader to focus quickly on those areas in which they are particularly interested.

References

1 NHS Executive (2005) *National Schedule of Reference Costs 2004*. Available directly at http://www.dh.gov.uk/PolicyAndGuidance/OrganisationPolicy/FinanceAndPlanning/NHSReferenceCosts/fs/en. From the DH homepage follow links for Policy and guidance, Organisation policy, Finance and planning, and NHS Reference Costs.
2 Curtis L and Netten A (2004) *Unit Costs of Health and Social Care 2004*. PSSRU, University of Kent, Canterbury. Also available at: http://www.pssru.ac.uk/uc/uc2004.htm.
3 British Medical Association and the Royal Pharmaceutical Society of Great Britain (2005) *British National Formulary*. 50. British Medical Association and The Pharmaceutical Press, London.

2 Techniques of economic appraisal

Introduction

Demand for healthcare will always outstrip the resources available to meet such demand. As such a state of scarcity will exist. A means of deciding which of the competing demands will receive resources and how much resource must be established. Health economics provides one such mechanism for allocating scarce resources.

This chapter will familiarise the reader with the reasons for undertaking an economic appraisal, the techniques of economic appraisal and outline the factors underlying choice of technique. Finally it will determine the steps necessary for undertaking and reviewing an economic appraisal.

Why evaluate?

Before undertaking any economic evaluation there must be an economic question posed. This centres around making a choice between two or more competing healthcare alternatives. Two key issues are often addressed in such questions. These are efficiency and equity. Efficiency is the search for the option that maximises benefit within a resource constraint. Equity seeks to ensure that all individuals are either given the same chance to benefit from healthcare, or are specifically targeted to redress previous inequalities.

The options considered within an economic evaluation

In the delivery of healthcare, there are at least four types of questions that an economic appraisal can address. These are: *what* type of healthcare; *where* is it delivered; *when* is it delivered; and to *whom* is it delivered?

What?

This concerns choices about what types of treatment should be given, if any, for particular conditions, i.e. a choice may be between a surgical intervention versus a drug intervention, or of one drug over another drug.

Where?

This concerns choices about where treatment should be provided, i.e. the choice between types of institutions (e.g. hospital and domiciliary care) or between different locations of institutional care. For example, should people with a mental illness be treated in hospital, in the community, or at home? Should paediatric outpatient clinics be held centrally at a large hospital or locally in smaller hospitals or clinics nearer to patients' homes?

When?

This concerns choices about when treatment should be available, i.e. the timing of care. Here, studies are aimed at assessing the best time to intervene in the course of a disease. Four relevant stages can be identified: vaccination before infection; screening to pick up the disease in the pre-symptomatic stages; curative treatment once the disease is clinically apparent; and finally rehabilitative or palliative care.

Who?

This concerns choices about to whom treatment should be given. This question asks which sections of the population should take priority. It may be classified by age, sex, social class or clinical condition. It is important to recognise that choices are being made implicitly on who should (and does) receive preferential treatment, who is kept waiting and who is denied; and it can be argued that better, more consistent decisions might be made if these values were made explicit. Choices in this area may go beyond the bounds of clinical need and efficiency, but instead focus upon issues concerning equity and policy decisions.

Viewpoint

The choice of the particular appraisal method will depend upon the viewpoint or perspective adopted and the information available to the decision maker. Viewpoint is important since it dictates the level of analysis and the type of costs and benefits that will be considered. Viewpoints include: society, such that all costs and benefits are considered; the NHS trust, such that costs only relating to the hospital and secondary care are considered (primary care costs would be excluded); or the patient, hence an evaluation may include the patients' travel costs.

Types of economic evaluation

The next section will outline the professional toolkit of the health economist in terms of the evaluation techniques. This will include the techniques of:

- cost minimisation analysis (CMA)
- cost benefit analysis (CBA)
- cost effectiveness analysis (CEA)
- cost utility analysis (CUA)
- cost consequences analysis (CCA)
- cost of illness studies (COI).

It will also outline the different data required for each type. The data required for each of these types of analysis will draw on the literature for measuring both benefits and costs. For a fuller consideration of benefits and costs the reader should refer to Chapters 7 and 8 respectively.

Economic evaluation is the comparative analysis of alternative courses of action in terms of both costs and benefits or outcomes. Economic evaluation serves two valuable purposes. First, it enables the identification of relevant alternatives and, second, it enables the prioritisation of those alternatives so as to permit the most efficient use of resources by enumerating the alternatives in terms of their costs and benefits.

Cost minimisation analysis (CMA)

Cost minimisation analysis is the simplest form of evaluation. It compares resource utilisation between alternative treatments known to have identical efficacy and calculates the net benefit in monetary terms. The most efficient option will be the least cost option. No ratio calculations are necessary and it is simply the comparison of one variable – cost – against itself.

Cost benefit analysis (CBA)

Cost benefit analysis compares the costs of a programme with the benefits of the programme, where all benefits are valued and stated in financial terms. The result may be expressed as a net benefit (or net cost) figure or as a cost:benefit ratio. Cost benefit analysis is often referred to as taking a broad or societal viewpoint. Although this may often be true, strictly speaking cost benefit analysis can be undertaken from a very specific viewpoint such as the individual hospital trust.

Cost effectiveness analysis (CEA)

Cost effectiveness analysis compares the costs of a healthcare intervention/programme to the natural units of that intervention or programme – for example, low-density lipoprotein in cholesterol or sight years saved in terms of visual acuity. Thus the eventual result of the analysis would be to arrive at a figure of cost per unit of benefit, rather than a direct comparison of costs and benefits, as is the case in CBA. In cost effectiveness analysis alternative interventions will be judged across equivalent outcome measures, i.e. the cost per case found or cost per life saved of one intervention compared to an alternative intervention.

Cost utility analysis (CUA)

In cost utility analysis the costs of a programme are compared to the health improvements attributable to the programme, where the health improvement is measured in Quality Adjusted Life Years (QALYs) gained. This signifies the overall utility within a programme and can be a composite of a number of different dimensions of health: including pain, mobility and social activities, combined with longevity. This is then expressed in terms of a single number or utility. The results are usually expressed as a cost per QALY gained.

Cost consequences analysis (CCA)

Cost consequences analysis is concerned with costs and benefits (both clinical and humanistic) in a study. It identifies all the consequent costs and benefits and may assign a value to each of these costs and benefits. It however presents the two sides of the equation separately, without evaluating the balance between costs and benefits. The comprehensive range of costs and benefits considered would make it difficult to find a common unit in which to express costs and benefits in terms of a single figure or ratio.

Cost of illness studies (COI)

Cost of illness studies attempt to estimate the cost of treating and managing a specific disease in society. They are sometimes referred to as burden of disease studies. This type of study takes a societal perspective, and as such should include both direct and indirect costs. They can provide important information to decision makers about expenditure in a given area. However, they should not be used to inform decision makers on what choices to make, as these types of study do not take into account the consequences of such expenditure.

Table 2.1 provides a summary of the different forms of economic evaluation. It details their units of enumeration in terms of costs and benefits and the final reporting unit.

Table 2.1 Economic evaluation summary

	Unit of cost measurement	Unit of outcome measurement	Evaluation result
Cost minimisation analysis	Money	Clinical effect measure or utility	Cost
Cost benefit analysis	Money	Money	Cost:benefit ratio or net cost/net benefit figure
Cost effectiveness analysis	Money	Clinical effect measure	Cost per unit of effect
Cost utility analysis	Money	Utility (QALYs)	Cost per QALY
Cost consequences analysis	Money	Multiple measures including clinical utility and economic effects	No explicit measure; costs and effects listed separately
Cost of illness studies	Money	Disease or illness	Cost

Good practice guidelines for economic appraisal

As well as undergoing safety and efficacy checks before a product gains a licence, many countries are now introducing an economic hurdle that a product must also overcome before it can be readily taken up by the market. Some countries now require health economic data as part of the dossier that must be submitted for pricing and reimbursement approval.

Many countries have established organisations that examine the economic implications of healthcare interventions. Some of these organisations and policy boards are non-mandatory and are merely an advisory guideline or body in a specific country. The first country to introduce a formal health economics requirement was Australia. More recently, some European countries, including Finland, Sweden and Norway, have introduced a formal requirement for economic evaluation for pricing and reimbursement if a premium price is required for a new product. There is no such requirement for economic evaluation for all products in the UK. However, should either an existing or a new technology be appraised by the National Institute for Health and Clinical Excellence (*see* Chapter 6), the economic implications of the technology and the (budgetary) impact on the National Health Service (NHS) will be considered along with the clinical effectiveness data.

A checklist for reviewing or undertaking an economic appraisal

Many roles in healthcare will require us to critically appraise others' work and to make choices and decisions based on the findings and conclusions of such work. Similarly, one may be in a position of commissioning work from others in healthcare to answer a particular question or to inform a decision.

Box 2.1 represents a simplified checklist adapted from Drummond *et al.* (2005).[1] The checklist will aid the reader in formulating both an economic appraisal and a critique of an economic appraisal. Each step will be addressed in turn and its key features highlighted.

Box 2.1

1 Objective
  (a) What questions does the study attempt to answer?

2 Viewpoint
  (a) What viewpoint does the study adopt?

3 Options
  (a) What alternative strategies are considered?
  (b) How did the author(s) go about generating alternatives?
  (c) Do you have any comments on the way the (treatment) choices have been set out?
  (d) Are there other choices that could (should) have been considered at the same time?

4 Benefit measurement
  (a) Are you happy with the way benefits have been listed and measured in the study?
  (b) If not, what method or approach would you propose?
  (c) If yes, are you content with the values derived?

5 Cost data
  (a) Are you happy with the financial estimates made?
  (b) Are the methods of valuation satisfactory?
  (c) Are any relevant costs omitted?

6 Medical data
  (a) Is the study based on reliable epidemiological, demographic and clinical evidence?
  (b) If not, what further information would you require?
  (c) Is such information available and, if so, where and from whom?

7 Risk and uncertainty
  (a) Does the study allow for:
    (i) uncertainty (or errors) in the expected costs and benefits?
    (ii) the differential timing of costs and benefits?
    (iii) the incidence of costs and the distribution of benefits within society?

8 Options appraisal and decision making
  (a) Finally, on the basis of the results presented in this study, would you feel confident in recommending a course of action to your health board?
  (b) If not, in what ways (other than those implicit in your answers above) would the study need to be modified or amplified in order to assist you in giving advice?

Source: Adapted version of Box 3.1 (pp. 28–9) from Drummond *et al.* (2005).[1] By permission of Oxford University Press.

Objective

There should always be a clear objective before undertaking a study. What is the issue or area to be studied? Questions such as 'which is the better product?' or 'is this procedure worthwhile?' are too vague. Objectives may include which drug is more cost effective than another drug or which is the most efficacious treatment (and at what cost). The reader should be able to easily understand the alternatives that are being compared, the characteristics of the study group (which may limit the application of the results), the perspective of the study, and the endpoint that is being used. Both costs and benefits should be measured. All these should become clear once a study objective has been set.

Viewpoint

As stated earlier it is important not only to specify clearly the study question at this point, but also the viewpoint or perspective of the study. Again this will define the costs and benefits chosen for measurement. Viewpoints include societal, national/governmental, purchaser, provider or patient. A study may present the health economic outcome for more than one viewpoint. A study by Cobos and co-workers[2] reported the cost effectiveness of different statins in treating hypercholesterolaemia in Spain from two perspectives: public financing, which included the direct costs incurred by the healthcare system, and societal, for which the authors included direct costs and labour costs, such as the time spent visiting the physician and days of work lost because of drug-associated adverse events.

Options

It is important to be confident that all the appropriate treatment options have been identified in any evaluation. Equally if any are omitted it is important to identify the reason why. The intention is that, to enable comparison of one's own practice to that within the study, the treatment options as such must be adequately described. The type of information that should be given is as follows:

- What will be evaluated?
- Where will care be delivered?
- Which clients will receive care?

- When will the care be delivered, in terms of prevention, treatment, rehabilitation or palliative care?

Benefit measurement

Outcomes may be measured in a number of different ways (*see* Chapter 7). The most meaningful benefits for the study must be identified, to ensure the most relevant change is analysed. The benefit chosen may range from a simple measure of effect – for example, a positive or negative test result – through to utility measures such as the EuroQol Five Dimensions tool (EQ-5D).[3] The type of benefit measure chosen will then drive the type of economic analysis undertaken – for example, cost effectiveness analysis or cost utility analysis. Benefits may be assessed directly from the patient, or estimated from the literature or alternative data sources such as existing audit databases for a patient group.

Cost data

A study may include different phases of treatment and the costs are likely to vary according to the phase. Similarly as with benefits, the costs measured are likely to vary with viewpoint. It is important to ensure that all the relevant costs for the study in question are identified and measured appropriately (*see* Chapter 8). Costs measured may include those borne by patients, by the healthcare system and by society in general; and are usually divided into direct (capital, staff and consumables) and indirect (earnings). It is important to check that the appropriate unit of measurement has been chosen for cost. If, for example, staff is the important cost driver, it may be necessary to measure staff time and apportion cost per minute rather than a daily average. In terms of the values for costs, they should be based on current market values; the currency and year for which costs are being calculated should be stated and be consistent throughout.

Medical data

The medical data forming the basis for the analysis must be valid, reliable and build upon the best available evidence. Sources of medical data should be clearly stated and consistency in reporting and base year must be observed. They must be based on validated and reliable trials, epidemiological studies or models. Questions to ask when using or comparing analysis based on the medical data include the following:

- If a study has used data from one population subset, is it valid to apply the results to more than that subset?
- Are the age groups consistent with the current analysis?
- Are there any special demographic or ethnic considerations?

A good practice guideline for reviewing the quality of reporting of clinical trials is the CONSORT Statement.[4]

Risk and uncertainty

Three key factors are raised in addressing this area:

- Has the study been adjusted for differential timings?[5]
- Is an adequate sensitivity analysis performed?
- Have distributional consequences been addressed?

Costs and benefits must be adjusted for differential timings, particularly when costs are likely to be incurred at a different time to when the benefits (such as life years gained) become apparent. In essence, we all exhibit a time preference for costs and benefits; this may be translated typically, as we prefer to incur our costs later and our benefits sooner. In terms of analysis all costs and benefits must be presented in terms of their current value. Costs and benefits may be discounted at the same rate or differential rates. However, there is no consensus on how much to discount, although generally a rate of between 3% and 8% per year is used. In the UK current recommendations are 3.5% for costs and 3.5% for benefits, the rates recommended by the Department of Health for NICE appraisals.[5]

A sensitivity analysis should be conducted if there is any uncertainty about the effectiveness and/or costs of the different procedures or programmes of treatment, in particular where assumptions have been used, such as the discount rate or different risk values. The first step is therefore to identify which are likely to be the most sensitive variables. The analysis is then performed by applying a variation to sensitive variables – to either the costs or the efficacy parameters – and the cost and benefit ratio is recalculated. Variables can be altered one at a time ('univariate analysis') or more than one variable can be altered simultaneously ('multivariate analysis').

Finally, mention should be made of the fact that the incidence of costs when compared with the distribution of benefits may be in directions that society will judge as inequitable. In other words, although a 'straight' cost benefit analysis might well produce a surplus of benefit over cost, nonetheless the resulting distribution of such rewards (and penalties) may be considered undesirable. It will quite often be appropriate to show how the costs and benefits are distributed among different organisations, sectors of the economy (private versus public sector), or individuals. Techniques may vary but all aim to identify the 'donor' and the 'recipient' so that policy makers can, if they so wish, take 'corrective action', e.g. to the financing of such services, to the methods of determining eligibility, or to the procedures for allocating such services to the population.

Options appraisal and decision making

A first question to be asked in this section is: did the study results and discussion include all issues of concern to users? Comparison with other studies and explanation of the differences should be made, although comparisons of studies should only be made if the methods are similar. Problems of generalisability arise, for example, because of diversity in patient populations or care delivery systems. Thus, application of study results between different countries is not always possible.

In cardiovascular health there are substantial differences in outcome between, for example, males and females, different age groups and those with different baseline values. The question is therefore can results from one subset of the population be applied to a different subset? For example, several studies have found that one statin may be most cost effective for patients at low risk or with a relatively small elevation in low-density lipoprotein cholesterol (LDL-C) level, while a different statin is more cost effective in high-risk patients, or those with a greatly elevated LDL-C level.[6,7] It is important that the results and assumptions are transparent so that they can be generalised and interpreted within a different setting.

Health economic data may not be easily transferable from one setting or country to another. Factors affecting transferability include demographics and epidemiology of disease, different treatment patterns, relative costs of treatment, methods for the delivery of healthcare, and the availability of resources. In order to transfer data from one setting to another, modelling methods may be used.

Discussion of the results of an economic evaluation should include comparison with other studies. The ability to compare the results of an economic study with other situations, illustration of how the results help in decision making, other important factors relevant to the decision under consideration and the feasibility of implementing the preferred option should also be discussed.

Health economics data are used by a variety of different decision makers. At a national level, economic data may be used to support national price listing and decisions on reimbursement. At a local or institutional level, they can be used to support formulary listings, inclusion in treatment protocols and to assist individual clinicians in their decision making. Consequently, many bodies are starting to integrate economic assessments into the decision-making process.

Although there is no magic formula for translating the results of evaluation into policy, the results of an economic evaluation will indicate the expected costs and benefits of interventions. This will tell the decision maker whether the costs incurred are likely to be justified by the benefits accrued from an intervention – in other words, which intervention will give the greatest benefit per unit of resource. While a health economics study is a useful tool, the decision whether to accept the intervention or technology is the responsibility of the stakeholder concerned.

Conclusion

This chapter has sought to establish the importance of economic evaluation and the areas to which economic evaluation is applicable. It has examined the special situation of healthcare and introduced some of the economic appraisal techniques available for undertaking economic evaluation. Finally, it has presented a key checklist for both undertaking and appraising an economic evaluation.

References

1 Drummond MF, Sculpher MJ, Torrance GW *et al.* (2005) *Methods for the Economic Evaluation of Health Care Programmes* (3e). Oxford University Press, Oxford.

2 Cobos A, Jovell AJ, Garcia-Altes A *et al.* (1999) Which statin is most efficient for the treatment of hypercholesterolemia? A cost-effectiveness analysis. *Clinical Therapeutics*. **21**: 1924–36.

3 EuroQol Group (1990) EuroQol – a new facility for the measurement of health-related quality of life. *Health Policy*. **16**: 199–208.
4 Moher D, Schulz KF and Altman D (for the CONSORT Group) (2001) The CONSORT Statement: revised recommendations for improving the quality of reports of parallel-group randomized trials. *JAMA*. **285**(15): 1987–91.
5 National Institute for Clinical Excellence (2001) *Guidance for Manufacturers and Sponsors: Technology Appraisals Process Series No. 5*. HMSO, London.
6 Bottorff MB and Tenero DM (1999) Pharmacokinetics of eprosartan in healthy subjects, patients with hypertension, and special populations. *Pharmacotherapy*. **19**(4Pt2): 73S–78S.
7 Hilleman DE, Phillips JO, Mohiuddin SM *et al*. (1999) A population-based treat-to-target pharmacoeconomic analysis of HMG-CoA reductase inhibitors in hypercholesterolemia. *Clinical Therapeutics*. **21**: 536–62.

3 UK national data

Introduction

Many costs used in economic evaluation will be potentially common across hospitals and geographical locations. Although it is preferable to use local costs where they exist, it is not always possible or practical to collect such costs. An alternative to using local costs and their sources may be to use national sources of cost data available. A combination of the two sources of costs – local and national – may be used. The key is that local resource use information should always be utilised and full advantage taken of this information.

Similarly, on the outcome side epidemiological information requires large datasets, particularly where events are rare, to guarantee the validity of findings. In such studies, it is therefore likely that patients will be drawn from several sites. Hence it is more appropriate to then apply national aggregate data sources for determining disease prevalence, for example, than outcome data derived from only a small number of patients. National cost data may then be applied to such epidemiological databases. The key as ever is to ensure that the assumptions used in either cost or outcomes (benefits) analyses are made explicit, thus enabling local decision makers to then substitute alternative data if they so wish.

This chapter discusses sources of cost and health outcome data available at a UK national level. Its explanation of cost data will cover secondary care including ward stays, hospital attendances and outpatient appointments, staff and drugs. Furthermore it will examine an approach for inflating costs over time. It outlines the system of Payment by Results (PbR), which applies average cost data to procedures across all NHS trusts in England and Wales. On the outcome side an example of a disease register is described. Disease registers can be useful for providing information on the extent of the global burden of the disease which can then be used to determine overall treatment costs. Further in terms of health outcomes, mortality rates and life expectancy are discussed and a range of social surveys considered.

NHS Reference Costs

NHS Reference Costs[1] are potentially one of the most useful cost sources since they include national average unit costs for NHS hospital care and community-based services in England and Wales. NHS Reference Costs are available on the Department of Health (DH) website at http://www.dh.gov.uk/PolicyAndGuidance/OrganisationPolicy/FinanceAndPlanning/NHSReferenceCosts/fs/en. Reference Costs are split into two sections: the National Schedule of Reference Costs (NSRC) and the National Reference Cost Index (NRCI). The National Schedule of Reference Costs provides national average unit costs for a vast range of treatments and procedures. The National Reference Cost Index ranks each NHS trust based on its casemix. Reference Costs provide the basis for the national tariffs currently being developed and the implementation of Payment by Results (PbR), which will be discussed at the end of the section.

National Schedule of Reference Costs (NSRC)

It is the NSRC or average costs for procedures that are the most useful to health economists. The coverage of the NSRC has expanded greatly since it first became available in 1998 to include not only inpatient care but also many specialist and community services. The hospital- and community-based services for which national average unit costs are provided are:

- elective inpatients
- non-elective inpatients
- day cases
- critical care
- outpatients (split between first and follow-up attendances)
- ward attenders
- regular day or night attenders
- radiotherapy
- specialist services such as renal dialysis, bone marrow transplants, spinal injuries and rehabilitation
- accident and emergency (A&E) services
- pathology and radiology services
- audiology services

- mental health services
- community nursing services
- district nursing and health visiting services
- direct access and community therapy services
- paramedic services.

Information on inpatient care, day cases and A&E services is available by Healthcare Resource Group (HRG) code, while other information on outpatient and ward attendances is split by specialty codes. Information has been further expanded to include additional costs for elective inpatients' excess bed days, and non-elective inpatients' excess bed days. This is the average cost for additional days in hospital for patients who have exceptionally long stays. It is an additional cost per day that only applies to the additional days beyond the trim point (determined by the DH and beyond the 95th percentile), and does not apply to additional days above the average but below the trim point.

In the NSRC and with the implementation of PbR it will no longer be possible to obtain an average bed day cost alone by specialty, or a ward-based cost. Unfortunately, only whole costs for procedures will be available, which take into account all the individual components of cost rather than enabling them to be attributed separately.

Reference Cost information is available by type of provider, i.e. NHS trusts, primary care trusts, Personal Medical Services plus (PMS+) pilots and non-NHS providers. For those wanting to perform more detailed analyses, a database of the source data from each of the organisations included is available on CD-ROM on request from the DH.

For each component of the services, the interquartile range (the unit costs attributable to the bounds of the middle 50% of NHS trusts) is given as well as the average unit cost. The total activity that figures are based on is also provided, be that the total number of finished consultant episodes (FCEs), or the number of treatments/ bed days/attendances. These can be seen in the extract from the section for elective inpatient care from Reference Costs 2004, as shown in Table 3.1.

Using NHS Reference Costs enables the researcher to quickly interpret resource data correctly without imposing an additional burden on the study or local trust. Appropriate cost data may not always be readily available at a local level. However, such national data can only ever provide average figures, which may differ from hospital to hospital depending on the nature of how the procedure is performed, and the general knowledge base of the hospital concerned. Similarly, each procedure will differ on a patient-by-patient basis, governed by the patients' medical condition and severity.

National Reference Cost Index (NRCI)

This single index compares the actual average cost of the casemix of each NHS trust with the cost of that casemix based on average unit costs. It is used primarily for setting unit cost targets for NHS providers. A trust with an index of 100 therefore has costs equal to the national average, while an organisation with an index of 120 has costs 20% above the national average. This is the guiding principle that is used in PbR, in that trusts will only be paid a national average cost for any procedure that they perform. It will enable trusts to determine their market position and overall efficiency.

Payment by Results (PbR)

The NSRC is being used to create a national tariff that covers admitted patients (elective and non-elective inpatients/daycases), outpatients and A&E services, and will be based on spells rather than FCEs. A spell is defined as one inpatient stay. The national tariff is a schedule of national prices that will be applied to every trust in the NHS. All trusts will receive the same payment for a specified HRG regardless of where they are in the country or any patient characteristics. Hence there will be no price differentials and hence no price competition. Currently there are trusts that have costs above tariff and some who have costs below tariff, and many trusts who are above tariff for some procedures and below tariff for others. PbR will be implemented by 2008, with many common procedures already having a tariff attached. Certain sectors such as mental health services and ambulance trusts will be excluded from PbR. More information on PbR can be found on the DH's website at http://www.dh.gov.uk/PolicyAndGuidance/OrganisationPolicy/FinanceAndPlanning/NHSFinancialReforms/fs/en.[2]

PbR negates the use of local cost data and means whatever the individual cost structure of each trust, the cost borne by the health

Table 3.1 Extract from the elective inpatient section of the NHS Trust Reference Cost Schedules (Appendix SRC1) from *Reference Costs 2004*

HRG code	HRG label	No. of FCEs	National average unit cost	Interquartile range of unit costs		No. of bed days	Average length of stay (days)	No. of data submissions
				Lower quartile	Upper quartile			
			£	£	£			
H01	Bilateral primary hip replacement	286	6061	4440	7233	3008	11	76
H03	Bilateral primary knee replacement	934	7056	4926	8219	9342	10	100
H04	Primary knee replacement	46 199	5313	4704	5938	399 690	9	166
H07	Primary or revisional shoulder, elbow, or ankle replacements	2711	4386	2921	4600	16 154	6	156
H08	Joint replacements or revisions, site unspecified	2835	3755	2450	4155	17 056	6	170
H09	Anterior cruciate ligament reconstruction	1209	2022	1409	2834	3168	3	115
H10	Arthroscopies	37 069	1206	867	1580	55 334	1	226

Source: Adapted from NHS Executive (2005), Appendix SRC1.[1]

service is the national tariff price where a tariff price exists. A trust that can increase its daycase load from traditional inpatient care, for example, can make potential cost savings. The implication is that there will be overall efficiency gains in healthcare with potentially shorter length of stays. Trusts that are above average cost will need to make cost savings; this may take the form of reductions in staffing levels.

Unit costs of health and social care

The Personal Social Services Research Unit (PSSRU) at the University of Kent produces an annual report on unit costs of providing care. This is singly one of the most important references available. A copy of this report is available on the PSSRU website at http://www.pssru.ac.uk/uc/uc2004.htm.[3] It covers both hospital- and community-based healthcare staff, as well as hospital attendances, services for specific groups, aids and adaptations for the home, and transport. Staff and hospital attendances are covered here; services, aids and transport are discussed in Chapter 5.

Staff

Staff costs are calculated using the same methods throughout; hence what follows here applies to all staff regardless of whether they are based in primary or secondary care. The components given for staff costs are salary, salary oncosts, qualifications, overheads, capital overheads and travel if applicable. For doctors, there is an additional component for ongoing training. The salary takes into account the proportion of staff receiving a London allowance, but does not adjust for other allowances or unsociable hours payments. It is based on a national average of salaries. Multipliers are also given to adjust costs for being exclusively in, or out of, London. Salary oncosts cover the employers' contribution to National Insurance and superannuation. The qualification cost is the cost of all training (pre- and post-registration) annuitised over the expected working life of the professional. For each cost element any additional notes such as where the information came from, or any assumptions made, are detailed. To illustrate, the unit costs for a specialist registrar are shown in Table 3.2.

Costs are attributed to the place of work, but where any employee works on more than one site, an element is given for travel costs.

Table 3.2 Unit costs for a specialist registrar

Costs and unit estimation	2003/2004 value	Notes
A. Wages/salary	£41 299 per year	Based on payment for 39.9 basic hours per week on duty (of which 89% are actually worked), and 30.7 additional hours per week (of which 43% are actually worked at a rate of 50% of basic rate). It does not reflect payments for London allowances.
B. Salary oncosts	£5054 per year	Employers' National Insurance plus 4% of salary for employers' contribution to superannuation.
C. Qualifications	£20 788 per year	The equivalent annual cost of pre-registration medical training and postgraduate medical education. The investment in training of a medical degree, one year spent as a pre-registration house officer and two years as a senior house officer have been annuitised over the expected working life of the doctor.
D. Overheads	£2450 per year	Comprises £2450 for indirect overheads. No allowance has been made for direct overheads because it is not possible to separate these from the cost of treatment.
E. Ongoing training	£3272 per year	Ongoing training is calculated using (provisional) budgetary information provided by the Medical Education Funding Unit of the NHS Executive relating to allocation of Medical and Dental Education Levy funds. Adjustment has been made to reflect assumed usage of educational facilities by this grade of doctor.
F. Capital overheads	£2569 per year	Based on the new build and land requirements of NHS facilities. Adjustments have been made to reflect shared use of administration and recreational facilities, including accommodation for night-time duties. Treatment space has not been included. Capital costs have been annuitised over 60 years at a discount rate of 3.5%. At 6%, the cost would be £3964.
Working time	37 weeks per annum	Includes 30 days annual leave and 10 statutory leave days. Assumes 30 study/training days, and 5 days sickness leave.
London multiplier	1.14 × (A to E); 1.49 × F	Allows for the higher costs associated with London compared to the national average cost. Building Cost Information Service and Department of the Environment.
Non-London multiplier	0.97 × (A to E); 0.97 × F	Allows for the lower costs associated with working outside London compared to the national average cost. Building Cost Information Service and Department of the Environment.

Unit costs available 2003/2004 (costs including qualifications given in brackets)
£20 (£29) per hour on duty; £29 (£42) per hour worked (includes A to F).

Source: Adapted from Curtis and Netten (2004), Schema 14.3, p. 183.[3]

Standard working hours a week are given, as are ratios of direct to indirect time on face-to-face patient contacts, clinic and surgery contacts and home visits, as appropriate for a particular healthcare professional. A variety of unit costs are then given. These generally include a cost per hour, per hour of patient contact, per hour in clinic contacts, per hour of home visiting, per consultation, and per home visit. To calculate the costs, direct and indirect overheads are detailed, as are capital overheads covering the need for expenditure on land and buildings.

The unit costs are broken down into great detail in this publication, allowing users to customise costs to their own situation – for example, when estimating the cost of a consultant. Information is given on qualification costs, and then all unit cost estimates are given with and without an element for this; such information then enables a researcher to manipulate the detail as best fits their local situation.

Hospital attendances

There is a short section giving unit costs for some hospital attendances. These include cost per bed day for several specialist care units and mental health services, cost per first outpatient attendance for some specialties and costs associated with community dietetics and dental services. The average unit cost and the interquartile range are given for each service. These are derived from Reference Costs.[1] It is likely that as the information reported in Reference Costs changes, and develops increasingly into the national tariff and PbR, the information contained in this publication on unit costs and how they are reported will also change.

DH Advance Letters: pay and conditions for medical staff

Salaries form one of the largest proportions of any evaluation or economic cost in healthcare. The DH Advance Letters for various categories of medical staff providing national salary scales and a national reference source for such data. These can be viewed on the web at http://www.dh.gov.uk/PublicationsAndStatistics/LettersAndCirculars/AdvancedLetters/fs/en. To find the Advance Letter required, select the appropriate health sector, and the letter referring to pay and conditions in the most recent year. Each letter shows the salary scales for each grade for that profession as well as the different increments for each grade.

NHS Logistics Authority catalogue

The NHS Logistics Authority was formed in April 2000, with the intention of improving efficiency and reducing the cost of delivering consumable healthcare products to NHS trusts. Their catalogue covers not only a vast spectrum of medical consumables required by hospitals, but also non-medical products ranging from catering equipment and food, to clothing, linen, stationery, electricals and furnishings. Different types of each item are detailed in the catalogue, and within each type are different pack sizes. More information can be found from their website at: http://www.logistics.nhs.uk.

Pharmaceutical costs

The main sources of cost information for pharmaceutical products are at a national level. The majority of spending on pharmaceuticals, however – some 79% – is in primary care.[4] Details on pharmaceutical costs will therefore be discussed in Chapter 5. A brief overview only is presented here. Three main sources exist for listing pharmaceutical costs: these are the *British National Formulary* (*BNF*),[5] the *Monthly Index of Medical Specialties* (*MIMS*)[6] and the *Drug Tariff*.[7] In brief:

- The *BNF* is published jointly by the British Medical Association and the Royal Pharmaceutical Society of Great Britain. It is a comprehensive drug guide for medications, and is updated every six months. It provides up-to-date information on all medications generally used in the UK, and reflects current best practice.
- *MIMS* is an alternative prescribing guide primarily used by GPs and sponsored by the pharmaceutical industry. It contains information on prescription medicines and over-the-counter (OTC) drugs. It is updated on a monthly basis and reflects the most up-to-date drug prices for branded drugs.
- The *Drug Tariff* is produced monthly by the Prescription Pricing Agency (PPA) on behalf of the DH. The PPA's role is that of a special health authority. It gives current prices for generic drugs, appliances, dressings, chemical reagents and oxygen therapy services for the home.

Further details on all these publications can be found in Chapter 5.

Hospital and Community Health Services (HCHS) inflation index

Prices rise over time because of inflation, and the HCHS inflation index is used to uplift older prices to present values. The HCHS inflation index measures inflation specifically for the health service. It is a weighted average of two inflation indices: the Pay Cost Index (PCI) and the Health Service Cost Index (HSCI). The PCI measures inflation relating to pay, while the HSCI measures inflation relating to prices.

When conducting an economic study, it is possible that all the data items and their respective costs may not be collected in the same year. Similarly, the year in which the researchers wish to present the data may differ from that in which it was collected. It is crucial that all cost data are presented consistently in the same year, and the inflation indices can be used to inflate any individual cost to its present value. The HCHS combined inflation index for pay and prices can be used to inflate costs, or the specific index for pay or prices can be used if that is more appropriate. Given that inflation relating to pay tends to exceed that relating to prices, it is important to use the most appropriate inflation index. Costs relating to staff time should be inflated using the PCI, whereas consumables should be inflated with the HSCI. Where costs are a combination of pay and prices, such as an outpatient appointment, it would be most appropriate to use the HCHS inflation index.

The PCI is a weighted average of increases in costs of all hospital and community health service staff groups. It is based on NHS pay awards.

Updated monthly, the HSCI measures the change in price of goods and services purchased by the health service. Forty-one services are indexed and these include medical and surgical equipment purchases, drugs, laundry/cleaning contracts, electricity and office equipment. The HSCI is calculated by weighting all the individual services according to the proportion of total expenditure that each represents. March 1993 is used as the base month (index = 100). The percentage increase over the last month and last 12 months are also included for comparison. The overall index can be used to uplift prices; or, if it is just required for a particular item such as electricity, it is more accurate to use the specific index for that service.

The HSCI has similarities with the retail price index; however, since the HSCI concentrates its calculations on health service goods only, it is a more accurate reflection of inflation for the health service than the retail price index.

The HCHS inflation index is available in *Unit Costs of Health and*

Social Care 2004.[3] This also provides the annual percentage increases for pay, prices, and pay and prices together which can be used to inflate costs to their present value.

The HSCI can also be found in the *Financial Matters* newsletter produced by the NHS Executive.[8] The HSCI figures are produced on a monthly basis and an annual summary table is produced at the end of each financial year (usually published the following May). Published with the annual summary table are annual percentage increases for pay, prices, and pay and prices together.

Disease registers

Disease registers catalogue the diagnosis and severity of a particular disease, its incidence and prevalence, and its geography. Such registers may vary in terms of their completeness and coverage. They may be maintained at a national, regional or district level. Disease registers provide information on the burden of a disease, which can be used to inform treatment decisions.

Disease registers are important in economic terms in that they provide details of the extent and severity of certain diseases. These data can be used to calculate the potential costs and the potential benefits both in terms of cost savings and quality of life from treating particular diseases. The national derived data on incidence and prevalence can be applied to local trials of, for example, drug A versus drug B to determine the likely population effects of different interventions in economic terms. Such registers can also be used to direct where resources should be focused in terms of both equity and need – that is, they may indicate where the greatest burden of disease is occurring. They may be used to help achieve the objective of economic efficiency; however, to achieve efficiency they must be linked to treatment and efficacy data.

A number of disease registers exist in the UK including diabetic registers, but by far the largest is the cancer registry. This is described next.

Cancer registers

In the UK, regional cancer registries regularly provide the Office for National Statistics (ONS) with their data. It is the national picture that will be presented here; regional boundaries are subject to change but the actual numbers of cases are not. Regional cancer registers are discussed further in *Harnessing Official Statistics* edited by Deana Leadbeter.[9]

There are many cancer datasets available from the 'health and care' section on the National Statistics website at: http://www.statistics.gov.uk/statbase/datasets2.asp.[10] They include information for individual cancer sites and summaries for major sites, on incidence, mortality (including age-standardised mortality rates) and survival; some of which may be split by gender, by five-year age band and by country of the UK and region of England.

Information on cervical and breast cancer screening programmes is available detailing, for instance, the percentage of the target population screened of various age groups, and giving age-standardised mortality rates. Screening programmes are discussed in greater detail in Chapter 5.

The most complete set of cancer information is available in the ONS publication *Cancer Trends in England and Wales, 1950–1999.*[11] It provides information on incidence, mortality and survival for all the major cancers. Importantly it notes that although prevalence data as such are not collected, cancer registrations are monitored up to death, so indirectly it is possible to estimate the number of people diagnosed with cancer who are still alive. This slightly underestimates the number of people with cancer, as those diagnosed before data became available in 1971 and still alive would not be included. Some of the information in this publication was updated in 2005.[12]

Appendix G[11] describes in detail the cancer registration system for England and Wales. Most registries collect large amounts of information about the patient, the tumour and the treatment, for use locally and nationally. There is a minimum dataset requirement for regional registries, who then forward the data to ONS. These items include:

- record type (new registration, amendment, deletion)
- demographic information
- incidence date
- date of death (if dead)
- site of primary growth
- type, and behaviour of growth
- multiple tumour indicator
- basis of diagnosis

- death certificate only indicator
- side
- treatment.

From 1993, there has been a phased introduction of the stage and grade of tumour. Initially this was introduced for breast and cervix. ONS optional information includes country of birth, ethnic origin, patient and head of household occupation and employment details, and whether the registration occurred from screening.

Cancer is the second largest cause of mortality in the Western world, hence is an important disease area for the economist. Economic evaluations are likely to cover the full spectrum of care from prevention (screening) to treatment to rehabilitation. Incidence figures are important in terms of prevention and screening. Often the economist, when evaluating a screening programme for example, will not only have to take into account the accuracy of the test, but the nature of the problem. It is therefore crucial to know both the incidence and prevalence of any particular cancer in order to understand the burden of the disease and the potential for the economics case. Equally when determining the effect of treatment, it is important to understand the natural history of the disease and hence the likely mortality with and without treatment. Trials in this field may be prohibitively expensive or numbers from a single site too small, and it is therefore important that national data exist to provide figures that individual decision makers, economists and analysts can then use.

Mortality rates

Mortality rates are often used as a measure of health. They can be used to project mortality without treatment, against a with-treatment comparison. Often it would be considered unethical to collect data on a no-treatment option but if such data exist nationally, they can present a baseline for analysis. In economic terms mortality rates can be used to direct resources to areas of greatest need, that is when the mortality rates by disease group are above the population average. This should be linked to treatment efficacy to determine the full economic argument for optimal treatment interventions.

Mortality rates are affected by the age structure of the population, making it awkward to compare mortality rates over time. This problem can be overcome by looking at Standardised Mortality Ratios (SMRs). This ratio (not an index) compares the expected number of deaths with the number actually observed, and is usually multiplied by 100 to avoid reporting decimal places. Hence the baseline ratio of an SMR is 100, when the number of deaths observed equals the number expected. Further information on the calculation of SMRs can be found in Bland (1987).[13]

The ONS publication *Mortality Statistics: general 2002*[14] provides information on deaths occurring in England and Wales, detailed by sex and age, and also by method of certification, and place of death. Some information is also split by geographical area. In particular, Table 3 provides SMRs for all persons, and for males and females separately from 1841 to 1999 – an extract of which is shown in Table 3.3. The base years are 1950–52, and it is obvious that mortality rates have reduced over time. *Mortality Statistics: general 2002*[14] also provides SMRs in greater detail by underlying cause, sex, and area of usual residence. *Mortality Statistics: general 2002*[14] provides a little information on infant and perinatal mortality and live and still births, but much more detailed statistics are available from the ONS publication *Mortality Statistics: childhood, infant and perinatal 2003.*[15] Datasets from both publications are available on the National Statistics website.[10] ONS mortality data are discussed further in *Harnessing Official Statistics.*[9]

Life expectancy

Life expectancy tables detail the remaining years of life at each age or with a specific diagnosis. Premature life years lost can be translated into potential life years gained that arise from treating the disease in question, and as such they can be used as a measure of health gain or longevity. They do not take into account quality of life. They are useful for predicting the gain in benefit or health (life years) with and without an intervention. This enables the incremental gain in terms of marginal benefit (where benefit is years of life) to be calculated and compared between two or more competing interventions. By combining effects or quality indicators of treatment with life years lost information, a measure of health outcome or loss can be constructed for each disease group. This measure of potential health gain from treatment can then be combined with cost to

Table 3.3 Deaths, death rates and SMRs for England and Wales

Period	Deaths			Crude rates per 1000 living			SMRs (1950–52 = 100)		
	Persons	Males	Females	P	M	F	P	M	F
1981–85	2 896 974	1 443 291	1 453 683	11.7	11.9	11.4	75	78	72
1986–90	2 861 323	1 407 628	1 453 695	11.4	11.5	11.3	70	72	69
1991–95	2 830 033	1 370 879	1 459 154	11.1	11.1	11.1	67	67	67
1996–2000	2 762 213	1 318 100	1 444 113	10.7	10.5	10.9	63	61	65
1981	577 890	289 022	288 868	11.6	12.0	11.3	76	80	73
1982	581 861	290 166	291 695	11.7	12.0	11.5	76	79	73
1983	579 608	289 419	290 189	11.7	12.0	11.4	75	78	72
1984	566 881	282 357	284 524	11.4	11.7	11.1	73	76	70
1985	590 734	292 327	298 407	11.8	12.1	11.7	75	77	73
1986	581 203	287 894	293 309	11.6	11.8	11.4	73	75	71
1987	566 994	280 177	286 817	11.3	11.5	11.1	70	72	68
1988	571 408	280 931	290 477	11.4	11.5	11.3	71	72	70
1989	576 872	281 290	295 582	11.4	11.5	11.4	70	71	69
1990	564 846	277 336	287 510	11.2	11.3	11.1	68	69	67
1991	570 044	277 582	292 462	11.2	11.2	11.2	68	69	68
1992	558 313	271 732	286 581	11.0	11.0	11.0	67	67	66
1993	578 799	279 561	299 238	11.4	11.3	11.4	69	69	69
1994	553 194	267 555	285 639	10.8	10.8	10.9	66	66	66
1995	569 683	274 449	295 234	11.1	11.0	11.2	67	66	68
1996	560 135	268 682	291 453	10.9	10.7	11.1	65	64	66
1997	555 281	264 865	290 416	10.8	10.6	11.0	64	62	66
1998	555 015	264 707	290 308	10.7	10.5	11.0	63	62	65
1999	556 118	264 299	291 819	10.7	10.4	11.0	63	61	66
2000	535 664	255 547	280 117	10.3	10.1	10.5	60	58	63
2001	530 373	252 426	277 947	10.1	9.8	10.4	59	57	62
2002	533 527	253 144	280 383	10.2	9.9	10.5	59	56	62

Source: Adapted from ONS (2004) Table 3.[14]

calculate the incremental cost and benefit differences between interventions.

Life expectancy at birth and selected ages by gender for Great Britain, together with other datasets and publications, are available from the population section of http://www.statistics.gov.uk.[10] The Government Statistical Service publication *Health and Personal Social Services Statistics* contains figures on life expectancy at birth and selected ages by gender for England. This is available at http://www.performance.doh.gov.uk/HPSSS/ in the Public Health section.

Every ten years the Government Actuary's Department (GAD) produces graduated life tables based on data obtained in a census year. Each year in between, however, they produce interim life tables based on population estimates and mortality data for the preceding three years. It is considered more robust to aggregate information from three years to increase the numbers involved, and hence reliability, rather than use a single year. Life expectancy estimates therefore are often quoted as three-year aggregate figures. Life expectancy at every age from 0 to 100, for males and females, and for the individual countries of the UK and as a whole, can be found on the GAD website at http://www.gad.gov.uk. These tables give the marginal life expectancy rather than the absolute value; that is, they represent the expected life left rather than the total expected life years.

Social Trends

Published annually by ONS, *Social Trends* provides a broad picture of the socio-economic state of Britain and covers areas as diverse as education, housing, crime and justice, and transport. Areas of most interest here include population statistics, health, income and expenditure. The current (2005) edition of *Social Trends 35* is available directly at http://www.statistics.gov.uk/socialtrends.[16]

The chapter devoted to health covers issues from diet and lifestyle, to life expectancy and mortality, and preventative medicine. Lifestyle indicators such as the amount of exercise taken, smoking habits, drug use and alcohol consumption are studied. Mortality rates from major causes are given, as well as death counts from accidents, suicide, and drug-related poisoning. Sexually transmitted infection counts are also included. There is information on the prevalence of treated heart disease, stroke, depression and insulin-treated diabetes obtained from the General Practice Research Database (more on this in Chapter 5). There is a range of information on cancer including standardised incidence rates, uptake of breast cancer and cervical screening, and death rates from breast and prostate cancer in Europe. Statistics on the uptake of childhood immunisation are also included. At the end of the chapter there are some useful contact details for various disease areas and surveys within ONS, and for other government departments. Many of the datasets in *Social Trends* are available on the National Statistics website.[10] *Regional Trends*[17] is another ONS publication describing the socio-economic state of Great Britain but the information is split into geographical regions. This therefore may be considered as an alternative or duplicate source.

Census

The Census is a survey of every household in the UK and is conducted every ten years. The last Census was held on 29 April 2001. The Census is the only survey of its kind to cover all households rather than attempting to obtain a representative sample. It collects information on each member of the household which includes age, gender, qualifications and occupation, social class, family structure, housing and amenities. The information collected is used by various government departments to inform policy making and aid the allocation of public expenditure. However, some of the information is useful for health economists, particularly again in targeting specific disease areas and predicting the burden of disease from which to then perform economic analysis.

Census information is available on the National Statistics website at http://www.statistics.gov.uk/census2001. Census material is also available free of charge for UK academics, once they have registered to use it; information can be found at http://www.census.ac.uk. The National Statistics website has results predominantly for England and Wales; further details for Scotland can be found at http://www.scrol.gov.uk/scrol/common/home.jsp, and for Northern Ireland at http://www.nisranew.nisra.gov.uk/census/start.html.

General Household Survey (GHS)

The GHS is an annual household survey conducted by the Social Survey Division of ONS, and sponsored by several other government departments including the Office of the Deputy Prime Minister, the Department for Work and Pensions and the DH. These departments use the information gained from the GHS to monitor the current situation and to assist planning and policy making. Each year interviews are conducted with around 9000 private households and everyone aged 16 and over in the household (some 16 000 adults).

Since April 2000 the GHS has consisted of two parts: the core questions are contained in the Continuous Survey, and occasional topic areas covered by trailers. The Continuous Survey consists of two questionnaires. The Household Reference Person is asked for household information on accommodation and facilities, and demographic information on residents. Then each adult household member is asked about their employment, income and pension, health, drinking and smoking habits. Trailers are additional sections perhaps only included once every five years. For example, it was agreed to include sections on social capital and informal carers during 2000/01, and contraception and hearing during 2002/03. Trailers are used when a particular sponsoring department requires information on an additional topic. More information on the survey can be found at http://www.statistics.gov.uk/ssd/surveys/general_household_survey.asp.

Although much of this information may not be of use to the economist, with increasing emphasis placed on the patient burden in healthcare, information such as that on informal carers could be very helpful. Further, such information could be used to inform the indirect costs of care through lost income and opportunities through illness for both the patient and their carers.

GHS data are available for each year since 1973, with the exception of 1997 and 1999. There is not only a wealth of information collected each year, but the continuity of the survey allows for comparisons over a substantial length of time. Further information, including the questionnaires, is available at: http://www.statistics. gov.uk/ghs. From 2005, *Social Trends*[16] is the primary means for publishing the results of the GHS, although datasets are still available on the National Statistics website.[10]

Conclusion

This chapter has detailed national sources of data that are useful for economic decision making. It has discussed the advantages of national data and outlined some of its potential uses, sources and applications. National data can be useful for providing a source of information for both cost and benefit data, and both have been discussed in this chapter. The choice of whether to use national data or local data, or a combination, is in the hands of the analyst or decision maker; the important point is to make all the actual data and the reasons for their use explicit to any reader. Local data give a better reflection of the local situation and issues; however, national data convey certain advantages both in the size of any potential datasets and in ease of access.

References

1 NHS Executive (2005) *National Schedule of Reference Costs 2004*. Available directly at: http://www.dh.gov.uk/PolicyAndGuidance/OrganisationPolicy/FinanceAndPlanning/NHSReferenceCosts/fs/en. From the DH homepage follow links for Policy and guidance, Organisation policy, Finance and planning, and NHS Reference Costs.
2 http://www.dh.gov.uk/PolicyAndGuidance/OrganisationPolicy/FinanceAndPlanning/NHSFinancialReforms/fs/en. From the DH homepage follow links for Policy and guidance, Organisation policy, Finance and planning, and Payment by Results.
3 Curtis L and Netten A (2004) *Unit Costs of Health and Social Care 2004*. PSSRU, University of Kent, Canterbury. Also available at: http://www.pssru.ac.uk/uc/uc2004.htm.
4 Office of Health Economics (OHE) (2003) *OHE Compendium of Health Statistics* (15e). Section 4, Family Health Services, Table 4.58. OHE, London.
5 British Medical Association and the Royal Pharmaceutical Society of Great Britain (2005) *British National Formulary*. **50**. British Medical Association and The Pharmaceutical Press, London.
6 *Monthly Index of Medical Specialties (MIMS)* (2005). August. Haymarket Medical, London.
7 Department of Health (2005) *Drug Tariff*. November. The Stationery Office, London.
8 HSCI in the *Financial Matters* newsletter: http://www.dh.gov.uk/PolicyAndGuidance/OrganisationPolicy/FinanceAndPlanning/fs/en,

select Financial Manual, and enter the Financial Manual website and select Newsletters/Financial Matters and Appendix 1 of the most recent Financial Matters.

9 Leadbeter D (ed.) (2000) *Harnessing Official Statistics*. Harnessing Health Information Series. Radcliffe Medical Press, Oxford.

10 National Statistics: http://www.statistics.gov.uk, and datasets section of the National Statistics website at: http://www.statistics.gov.uk/statbase/datasets2.asp.

11 Quinn MJ, Babb PJ, Brock A, Kirby EA and Jones J (2001) *Cancer Trends in England and Wales, 1950–1999*. Studies on Medical and Population Subjects No. 66. The Stationery Office, London. Also available at: http://www.statistics.gov.uk/downloads/theme_health/cancertrends_5099.pdf.

12 Rowan S, Wood H, Cooper N and Quinn M (2005) *Update to Cancer Trends in England and Wales 1950–1999*. Available at: http://www.statistics.gov.uk/downloads/theme_health/CancerTrendsUpdates.pdf.

13 Bland M (1987) *An Introduction to Medical Statistics*. Oxford University Press, Oxford.

14 Office for National Statistics (ONS) (2004) *Mortality Statistics: general 2002*. Series DH1 No. 35. The Stationery Office, London. Also available at: http://www.statistics.gov.uk/downloads/theme_health/DH1_35_2002/DH1no35.pdf.

15 Office for National Statistics (ONS) (2005) *Mortality Statistics: childhood, infant and perinatal 2003*. Series DH3 No. 36. The Stationery Office, London. Also available at: http://www.statistics.gov.uk/downloads/theme_health/Dh3_2003/DH3no36.pdf.

16 Office for National Statistics (ONS) (2005) *Social Trends*. **35**. The Stationery Office, London. Also available at: http://www.statistics gov.uk/socialtrends.

17 Office for National Statistics (ONS) (2004) *Regional Trends*. **38**. The Stationery Office, London. Also available at: http://www.statistics gov.uk/downloads/theme_compendia/Regional_Trends_38/rt38.pdf.

4 Secondary care data

Introduction

This chapter will examine the wealth of data held within an NHS trust. It will consider the linkage between the various systems within the hospital and with national data and information systems. Such systems utilise much trust data to form the larger national datasets.

The chapter first examines the trust-based systems that feed into national data, such as Hospital Episode Statistics and waiting list data. It then moves on to look at the data that relate to specific departments or specialties such as accident and emergency medicine, pathology, radiology and outpatient systems. It will further introduce the reader to topics that will be taken up in more depth in later chapters such as pharmaceutical costs.

Hospital administration systems (HAS)

Specifically the administration systems of a hospital contain individual records of patient information. Within the broad heading of a hospital administration system, such systems are often more specifically referred to as patient administration systems (PAS). These may be used to compile the statistical information that is important for analysis purposes. The HAS feeds into Hospital Episode Statistics (HES) and ultimately through to the national Reference Costs (*see* Chapter 3).

The HAS details each patient's hospital number, NHS number, full name and address and their GP. Administration systems can provide dates when the patient was admitted and discharged if they were an inpatient, or give dates of outpatient appointments and the treatment given. It should detail who they saw, the grade of staff, and which consultant. As with the HES system described in the next section, each individual consultant episode of care for an individual's stay in hospital is detailed separately.

The use of the HAS system can be an efficient way of accessing key data on patients in any particular study. If, for example, a randomised controlled trial (RCT) is being performed that requires data from patients in a local hospital, providing the trial patients can be identified, information on aspects such as length of stay can be accessed through the HAS system. This is rather than necessitating a separate field on the case report form in the RCT (*see* Chapter 8). Other useful fields include those around operation and diagnosis. All operations and diagnoses are recorded according to whether the patient is treated on an inpatient, daycase or outpatient basis. They are classified according to Office for National Statistics (ONS) codes for operations and procedures[1] and the International Classification of Diseases (ICD)[2] codes for diagnosis. It would therefore be possible to identify all the patients who had a primary hip replacement between August 2004 and September 2005.

The hospital administration system is therefore a useful source of raw data that can be used to provide activity and resource data within a study. The number of re-admissions, for example, may provide proxy outcome data. Accessing such data would still require ethical consent, even in a retrospective study.

Hospital Episode Statistics (HES)

The HES system (*see* Chapter 3 for further details) takes the data provided by the PAS system and provides an aggregated anonymised database that can be used to interrogate any of the fields collected within the HAS data. HES is a national information system that is dependent on using local patient data.

HES provides much information on inpatient care.[3] It is a records-based system on each patient episode in the hospital. Each record relates to one patient's period of care under a particular consultant during an inpatient stay. Hence it is possible to have more than one record for a stay in hospital if a patient changes consultant. Information collected includes a patient's age, date of admission and details of any operation or procedures. HES amalgamates records from PAS from all NHS trusts in England. Private hospitals are not included, but private patients treated in NHS hospitals are included. HES is managed by the Statistics Division of the Department of Health (DH). Further summary information on hospital activity can be found in the Hospital Activity Data.[4]

Although it is not possible to access the raw data as these are confidential patient records, many summary tables are published that allow questions to be answered while maintaining individual patient confidentiality. This standard data can be accessed from the Health and Social Care Information Centre at: http://www.hesonline.nhs.uk.[3] This provides information analysed by diagnosis, operation, Healthcare Resource Group (HRG), consultant specialty, NHS trust and strategic health authority. It is possible to compare data such as length of stay, waiting times, and demographic details across trusts.

As with all systems, there are areas that HES does not cover. It is not possible to look at drugs prescribed in hospital. It is also important to recognise that while the number of treatments undertaken can be determined, little information is available on their effectiveness.

It is worth pausing to consider an important subsection of the data contained within HES, which is data on waiting lists.

Waiting list data

This can be linked to GP data to detail every referral by general practice to each specialty. It is envisaged that future systems will synthesise more completely secondary and primary care data. Waiting list data can be classified by specialty and diagnosis. Waiting list data can specifically be found on the performance section of Hospital Activity Data on the DH website.[5] Waiting list data are a useful indicator of demand. Used alongside output data, they can further be used as an indicator of efficiency and throughput.

Numbers and time spent waiting by condition and by age can be used as a measure of burden of disease or benefits forgone by waiting. Short waiting times yield potential benefits to patients sooner rather than later.

Caveats should be applied to using waiting list data so that it is not used in a cavalier fashion. Researchers must be clear regarding the criteria for admission onto a waiting list. Long waits, for example, may discourage GPs from referring cases at all; hence a considerable unmet or undiagnosed burden of disease may exist in any locality.

Table 4.1 shows a sample of the waiting list data captured by each trust for first outpatient attendance. Such data can help establish a demand-side picture or burden of illness within a population.

Table 4.1 Outpatients' wait for first attendance by specialty, England summary

		Number of referral requests for first outpatient appointments		GP written referrals only							
				Effective length of wait from receipt of GP written referral request to first outpatient attendance (weeks)					Not yet seen at the end of quarter who have been waiting (weeks)		
Specialty code	Specialty name	GP written	Other	0 to <4	4 to <13	13 to <17	17 to <21	21 and over	13 to <17	17 to <21	21 and over
100	General surgery	303 036	69 109	113 017	121 317	25 069	1650	206	2281	5	40
101	Urology	105 387	33 758	26 859	43 559	12 249	1088	89	1387	7	35
110	Trauma & Orthopaedics	233 349	259 948	35 888	109 753	47 946	5168	449	4871	100	897
120	ENT	211 535	60 430	44 106	92 758	31 340	1814	115	2793	–	13
130	Ophthalmology	204 230	118 581	41 969	95 342	37 148	2233	219	3983	8	26
140	Oral surgery	97 602	36 831	19 570	45 712	14 119	1144	62	2107	1	–
160	Plastic surgery	30 689	25 154	6 484	15 091	5 282	803	15	620	19	255
170	Cardiothoracic surgery	824	9 275	409	201	30	1	–	3	–	–
301	Gastroenterology	47 278	18 502	9 258	17 287	5 965	606	24	881	10	16
320	Cardiology	82 251	45 824	28 687	30 304	9 753	735	150	1103	8	15
330	Dermatology	183 076	28 851	47 998	79 406	25 366	1801	120	2354	12	73
361	Nephrology	6 784	5 363	1 379	3 622	656	122	6	64	–	–
410	Rheumatology	56 413	16 977	9 800	29 692	9 529	717	75	952	2	2

Source: Adapted from Department of Health (2005).[6]

Healthcare Resource Groups (HRGs)

Healthcare Resource Groups attempt to link financial data by specialty and by procedure to resource usage and ultimately cost. HRG analyses can provide a useful source of average costings. HRGs are compiled by the Casemix Service of the NHS Health and Social Care Information Centre from 10.2 million records of all NHS inpatient episodes in England. HRGs are cases grouped into clinically meaningful categories and represent roughly equal levels of healthcare resource consumption. National and local figures are available for each group. Problems occur when the disease or procedure in question is not assigned to a HRG. Work is currently being undertaken to extend the HRG exercise into areas such as outpatients. HRGs in A&E medicine were published in 2001. HRGs are a way of top level allocation of costs to specialties.

Strategic and Financial Framework

Each trust maintains a broad financial forecasting and planning document that details overall performance against planned and projected performance. This is recorded as the Strategic and Financial Framework return sent to the DH. This is described more fully in Bullas and Ariotti, *Information for Managing Health Care Resources.*[7] It contains a large amount of top level or aggregate data. Both primary and secondary care information are included. A particular focus is in terms of national priorities. Separate sections are therefore included on cancer, heart disease, mental health and older people. The document is useful for establishing potential demand for services and burden of illness. Similarly, it can reflect how well demand is matched to supply.

Linkage between hospital and primary care data

The links between data held by GPs only and that shared between hospital trusts and primary care have improved in recent years. Data accessible to the trust now include the following from primary care: demographics, consultations, diagnoses (e.g. coronary heart disease), referrals, blood tests and medications. This enables a fuller picture to be established regarding the burden of disease and likely demand in any community. The identification of primary care data (for example, medications) enables a better resource profile to be determined for each patient by diagnostic category.

Accident and emergency (A&E) systems

Accident and emergency systems may vary in their design and manufacture but as standard they record attendance data, waiting time, diagnosis and triage category. Attempts have been made to link triage data with estimates of resource use by triage category. This can hence be used for financial planning purposes. Such systems can be used to identify peaks and troughs in demand for A&E services and again may be a useful planning tool when considering manpower and staffing decisions.

Theatre systems

Theatre systems provide detailed information on the type of operation, and the associated resource consequences. Theatre systems record codes for operations, sites (i.e. arm, leg) and the side of the patient being operated on (e.g. left or right). The operation codes come from the *Tabular List of the Classification of Surgical Operations and Procedures*,[1] and hence should link back to the PAS and HES systems.

The names of the surgeon and the anaesthetist are recorded, and the number of staff present in theatre. This can be misleading in terms of staff time as although eight staff may be listed they may not be present throughout the whole of the operation. The times for anaesthetics, in theatre and in recovery can be used as a proxy for staff time. In addition the consumables used in the operation are listed – for example, anaesthetic gases and blood. Using the gases in combination with anaesthetic time, for example, would allow the total cost for anaesthetics to be calculated.

The theatre system further records the number of theatre clinics proposed and cancelled. This enables a record to be kept of overall operating theatre efficiency and downtime. It can be used to investigate throughput and efficiency.

Pathology systems

Pathology systems record detailed information on tests requested for patients. They describe whether a single test was performed, or several were done as part of a profile. It details from where, and from whom the request came – be it a consultant or GP, in the same hospital or another, at an outpatient appointment, or at the patient's general practice.

Obviously the systems record test results. However, without something to compare this to, many of these results would be meaningless. Normal ranges are included for comparison. The system looks up the patient's sex and age, and attributes the appropriate normal range to the patient group. Systems will often flag abnormally high or low values, or conspicuously erroneous values.

Individual specialties will be able to provide much information on the costs of tests and procedures in their area. Pathology directorates can provide test costs for the departments within them such as biochemistry, haematology, histology, and microbiology. It is important to ascertain what is included in these costs as this may vary from trust to trust. Costs for procedures like a blood test will often include elements for the consumables, overheads and time taken to analyse the blood in the laboratory, but not the nurses' time to take the blood, or any consumables used on the ward, for example.

Staff costs

The finance department at each individual trust will be able to provide many local costs. These will include staff costs by grade, with an element for employment oncosts (employers' contribution to superannuation and National Insurance), and may include a local apportionment for overheads, and sickness and absence. Each trust is now responsible for local pay bargaining and hence wages are set for a locality. Broadly, with the exception of London weightings, these salaries will be similar across trusts, but care should be taken to use the appropriate salaries from the trust concerned in any study or analysis. Where seniority grades apply – for example, in nursing the grade ordering of A through to I (where I is the most senior), and in physiotherapy the titles of senior I and II – such grade ordering will be consistent across the country. When assigning a staff cost to any intervention it is important to be clear about the elements of time to be included. Staff time may relate to time spent directly with a patient and may include elements of non-patient-contact time (for example, administration).

Ward costs

Finance departments should be able to provide detailed costs for each individual ward. They can provide individual costs for the elements of direct ward costs such as the number and grade of staff, dressings, syringes, bed hire, as well as uniforms, printing and stationery. Similarly, individual costs are available for overheads such as catering, estates, finance, laundry and the pharmacy. There will also be an element for medical staff (consultants, registrars and junior doctors). All this information is totalled together, and can be divided by the total number of bed days provided by the ward, to give a detailed average cost per bed day.

It is often useful to be able to allocate costs to a specific type of ward. Intensive care unit ward costs, for example, will be considerably more than for a surgical inpatient ward, which in turn will be greater than a 'step down' or rehabilitation ward. If patients stay in different types of ward, a truer picture can be established of the resources for the elements of a patient's length of stay by ward type, rather than assuming one average cost throughout.

Table 4.2 provides an example of the type of resources quantified within ward-based costing. The contents are only examples of what might be included for a typical ward, hence the total figure gives an indicative amount for a ward cost over a year, rather than a summation of the figures presented. The total ward cost per annum can then be combined with total annual midnight bed occupancies to yield an average cost per bed day. The advantage of having this detail is that adjustments can be made to give a more accurate picture for particular circumstances. If more detailed information has been collected on a particular aspect (for instance, nurses' time) then the nursing staff elements can be stripped out, and the average ward-based costs replaced by more accurate estimates.

Pharmaceutical costs

Although many pharmaceutical costs will be incurred in primary care, pharmaceutical prescribing in the secondary sector is an important cost driver. Equally, drug regimes initiated in secondary care are highly influential in the eventual prescribing patterns in primary care. A number of sources exist for obtaining data and costs

Table 4.2 An indicative proforma of ward-based costs

Item	Cost per annum (£)
Direct ward costs	
Nurse grade D	136 710
. . .	. . .
. . .	. . .
Nurse grade F	120 654
Bedpans	2089
. . .	. . .
. . .	. . .
Syringes	4870
Staff uniform and clothing	831
. . .	. . .
. . .	. . .
. . .	. . .
Overheads	
Catering	75 012
Chaplaincy	4100
. . .	. . .
. . .	. . .
Estates	26 094
. . .	. . .
Total	2 506 365

for pharmaceutical entities; these will be described in Chapter 5. These data are useful for making national comparisons. It should not be forgotten, however, that individual hospitals and centres may negotiate special deals and discounts on the drugs that they purchase. Hence a large cancer centre may purchase sufficiently large quantities that the price they pay is less than in a standard district general hospital. Although it is important to be able to make national comparisons the local analyst may wish to use local prices; the choice of cost or price used should be clearly stated so that readers may interpret and apply the costs and as such the results correctly.

Outpatient costs

Outpatient costs will be available by specialty from trust finance departments, and will be split into first and follow-up appointment costs. New outpatient appointments are allocated a higher cost than follow-up appointments. It is deemed that more staff time and subsequent biological tests or X-rays will be undertaken at a new appointment. Subsequent appointments, unless complications occur, may mostly consist of minimal staff time and the use of a consulting room and administration.

Radiology costs

Radiology costs for procedures such as a chest X-ray, ultrasound scan and MRI (magnetic resonance imaging) scans will be available from the imaging directorate of an individual trust. More generally they are broken into seven Körner bands A–F, with most bands split into further subsections. The bands are translated into the workload required for each X-ray type and as such can be related to a resource cost for each band. The resource costs by band are recorded in the National Schedule of Reference Costs.[8]

Further work on the costs of radiology is available from work that is undertaken by benchmarking companies such as Newchurchltd.[9] These present median cost and interquartile ranges for chest X-ray, barium enema, CT (computed tomography) of abdomen and pelvis with contrast, MRI lumbar spine and ultrasound of abdomen, based on a sample of 60 trusts.

Physiotherapy and occupational therapy costs

Physiotherapist and occupational therapist time is recorded and allocated on a sessional basis. A specific or commercial system for recording such data is often not in place. Sessions are allocated in terms of the grade of therapist, usually in 15- or 20-minute slots, with more complex sessions allocated double slots. The allocation of time in terms of slots rather than on an actual per-minute basis is an important factor in terms of costing a therapist's time. Since all consultations are allocated in terms of whole sessions, even if the session finishes early or the patient doesn't turn up, it is not possible to use this time on additional patients. Similarly, the whole period of time must be assigned to the care of the patient to whom the slot was allocated, whether the patient is present or not.

Trust-specific databases

A trust, or an individual consultant within a trust, may develop a very specific expertise or interest. This may result in highly detailed and highly specialised databases being established in any individual trust. They may arise purely out of a personal interest by an individual within the trust or because of a larger study, trial or sponsorship. Often such databases are highly detailed and contain a rich breadth of data around a specific disease, e.g. breast cancer or a patient cohort. They may provide data unavailable elsewhere.

A problem with such databases is that they may not be subject to any nationally recognised validation or data definition systems. They may be so highly specialised and specific to a particular hospital or population that the data and results obtained from them may not be easily translated to a more general population.

Casenotes

Although much routine information is indeed stored on specific computer packages, e.g. patient administration systems, there will sometimes be specific information required either for a study or to answer a management question that will require the individual hand-searching of medical records. This is obviously a time-consuming process hence not an approach to be undertaken lightly. Case records, however, may contain a much greater level of detail about treatment procedures and consequences than are available from computer records, and thus they can be invaluable in establishing the true resource and benefit profile of care delivered to an individual, or group of patients.

Conclusions

Many of the data sources discussed in this chapter are invaluable in enabling the costs incurred by an NHS trust in delivering patient care to be calculated. They cover a broad number of categories from accident and emergency services to theatre systems and can provide costs for all cadres of staff from physiotherapists to nurses. Routine data sources can provide a wealth of resource and activity data for researchers without them having to establish their own databases. Similarly trusts hold specialist data that can be a unique and invaluable source for economic analysis. Care of course should be exercised to ensure that when a number of datasets are used, the definitions and information provided by such data sets are comparable.

References

1 Office for National Statistics (ONS) (1990) *Tabular List of the Classification of Surgical Operations and Procedures*. Fourth Revision Consolidated Version. HMSO, London.

2 World Health Organization (WHO) (1992) *International Statistical Classification of Diseases and Related Health Problems.* 10th Revision. WHO, Geneva.
3 Health and Social Care Information Centre (2005) *Hospital Episode Statistics.* http://www.hesonline.nhs.uk.
4 Department of Health (2005) *Hospital Activity Data.* http://www.performance.doh.gov.uk/hospitalactivity/.
5 Department of Health (2005) *Hospital Waiting List Statistics.* http://www.performance.doh.gov.uk/waitingtimes/index.htm.
6 Department of Health (2005) *Hospital Waiting List Statistics, Quarter 4 2004/05.* http://www.performance.doh.gov.uk/waitingtimes/2004/q4/qm08_y00.html.
7 Bullas S and Ariotti D (2002) *Information for Managing Health Care Resources.* Harnessing Health Information Series. Radcliffe Medical Press, Oxford, pp. 152–4.
8 Department of Health (2005) *NHS Reference Costs 2004*: Appendix SRCI. http://www.dh.gov.uk/assetRoot/04/10/55/53/04105553.xls.
9 Newchurchltd (2002) *Radiology Benchmarking Report 2001.* Newchurch, London.

5 Primary care data

Introduction

This chapter examines the use of data and information relating to primary care. While structured and systematic data collection in this area is not as advanced as the acute sector and national sources, useful material is obtainable for the analyst. Primary care is important in its own right, but it is also the gateway to secondary care. There are moves to integrate electronic records between the primary and secondary care sectors, but this has not happened as yet.

New NHS information systems have concentrated more closely on integrating primary care information with secondary care information. Such improved links will make it more viable to monitor, track and evaluate the whole patient journey from first contact with primary care, to any secondary and tertiary care referrals and subsequent continuing primary care management. As primary care and GPs have become not only the gatekeepers to medical care but also the budget holders, it is imperative that good information systems are established in this area. In the past where GPs have largely been sole traders operating on behalf of relatively small populations compared to hospital trusts, it has been difficult to establish a coherent and comprehensive network of GP information systems. The establishment of primary care trusts (PCTs) helps to some degree to reduce this problem.

This chapter will examine some of the sources of information relating to primary care. A large database of patient information from general practice, the General Practice Research Database, is considered first. The University of Kent's important publication, *Unit Costs of Health and Social Care*, which provides costs associated with residential and community care services, is described, as are sources of costs for pharmaceuticals. Other services provided in primary care such as vaccinations and screening programmes are discussed.

General Practice Research Database (GPRD)

The GPRD[1,2] is the world's largest computerised database of longitudinal patient information from general practice. It began in 1987. Detailed clinical data are collected by individual practices and entered into the database in a standard format. Around 300 general practices from all over the UK forward their anonymised data to the GPRD Group based at the Medicines and Healthcare products Regulatory Agency[3] (MHRA), who manage the database on behalf of the Department of Health (DH). Data are forwarded every six weeks or so. Currently the GPRD holds information on approximately 5% of the UK population.

Major illnesses, the diagnosis and outcome of any procedures performed, medications and any adverse reactions, childhood illnesses and pregnancy data must all be collected for each patient, as well as demographic data. Information on ethnicity is not recorded. There are strict regulations on data quality that must be adhered to by the participating practices. A minimum of 95% of the required data must be entered; otherwise practices are removed from the database. Routine validation checks are carried out to maintain these high standards.

A database containing this much information (several million patients followed for as long as 12 years) is an invaluable resource. Its key use has been in the area of drug safety. If a clinician reports a potential adverse side effect of a drug, the GPRD quickly provides a large cohort of patients taking the same medication. This cohort can be studied to ascertain if adverse effects are frequent, severe or prolonged and identify sectors of the group at increased risk. This is more rapid and much less costly than a dedicated randomised controlled trial.

The database is extremely valuable in providing a longitudinal data source linking patient events and prescribing to long-term outcomes. This is useful when attempting to predict the long-term effect of treatments that may only be performed over a relatively short time period such as a few years. It has further potential use in Phase III and IV pharmaceutical trials in terms of clinical and economic evaluation. The database can be a valuable resource in areas such as drug utilisation, health outcomes, and pharmacoeconomics. The script data could be combined with standard drug doses and costs and with the outcome data, to inform economic decision making on both costs and outcomes of prescription decisions.

Problems exist in that the data are not complete across time periods and certain data items have changed as the database has progressed. Over time, additional variables may become important disease predictors. For example, levels of cholesterol are now determined by high-density lipoprotein and low-density lipoprotein readings. These items have been added to the GPRD and can be used to predict long-term outcomes from introducing statin therapies. To become a fully comprehensive epidemiological database it is likely that further changes will be required to the GPRD. Incidence of certain diseases can be higher in some ethnic groups – for example, the higher incidence of diabetes in Asian populations. These links and the potential effects on prescribing patterns cannot currently be identified within the GPRD. If this became possible it would enable actions to be targeted towards certain ethnic groups as there may be medical grounds for altering prescribing patterns.

Some information is accessible free of charge from the GPRD website at http://www.gprd.com. Scale and quality reports allowing researchers to determine whether the GPRD could meet their needs, and sample patient profiles, as well as some Office for National Statistics (ONS) key health statistics are readily available. Further access to the GPRD is expensive. Access to the data is restricted to licensed users, who are required to have undergone training, which also incurs a fee.

Key Health Statistics from General Practice

The ONS publication, *Key Health Statistics from General Practice*,[4] shows how data from the GPRD can be used. The latest (1998) version is available at http://www.statistics.gov.uk/products/p4863.asp. This contains prevalence rates for major diseases, outpatient referral rates by clinical specialty, prescribing patterns and gives information on disease management by looking at the prescription of specific drugs for major disease areas. All this information is available for England and Wales; parts are also available by country and region, by ONS area classification, and by deprivation category.

Unit Costs of Health and Social Care

This is one of the most important sources of unit costs of care, and is produced annually by the Personal Social Services Research Unit (PSSRU) at the University of Kent and funded by the DH. It covers services for many vulnerable groups in the community: older people, those with mental health problems or learning difficulties, those who misuse drugs/alcohol, people with disabilities and children and their families. Unit costs are provided for doctors, nurses and professionals allied to medicine in both the hospital and community setting. Community-based staff across social care and educational support are also included. Other services covered are hospital attendances, ambulances, wheelchairs, and aids and appliances. A section covering services for children in care has been added recently. *Unit Costs of Health and Social Care 2004*[5] is the twelfth volume, and is freely available at http://www.pssru.ac.uk/uc/uc2004.htm.

Many costs used in economic evaluations are potentially common across geographical locations. This is particularity true of primary care costs where the system is more standardised than within the hospital setting. The PSSRU specialises in obtaining such costs on a national basis. Where primary care resources are used, but are not the main focus of a study, use of these unit costs may be considered to be both appropriate and accurate. If two hospital interventions are compared, there may be associated GP visits, and GP costs based on an average consultation time could be assigned. Where a study has a major primary care focus, if two competing interventions have differential amounts of GP time attributed to them, it is crucial to measure the time to undertake the intervention per patient. However, the unit costs for each minute of GP time with a patient (based on national data on salaries and overheads etc.) can then be applied to such times. Hence evaluations may use national cost data, local cost data or a combination of the two.

Hospital staff and attendances from this publication were discussed in Chapter 3. The unit costs provided for community care are described here. The cost of staff time is discussed first, then services for groups with special needs, followed by sections on transport, and aids and adaptations for the home. The examples used are intended to give a flavour of the manner in which costs are built up.

Staff

Staff costs for those working in the community are discussed here. The examples for calculating staff costs given in Chapter 3 for hospital staff can further be applied to those working in the community. It can be seen from Chapter 3 that the components for staff costs are salary, salary oncosts, qualifications, overheads, capital overheads and travel. The same method is applied to salary costs for professionals working in the community setting such as GPs, district nurses, health visitors, practice nurses and community-based professionals such as physiotherapists and speech therapists. The costs obtained are adjusted for factors such as location – for example, whether the visit took place at the surgery or the patient's home.

Services

This publication includes a wide range of unit costs for residential services for children, the elderly, those with learning difficulties, mental health problems, and those who misuse drugs/alcohol. Broadly speaking, each residential service covers the same cost areas. Costs are split into four sections: capital, revenue, health service and other costs. Capital costs comprise buildings and oncosts. Revenue costs cover elements for care staff and management salaries; catering, domestic services and utilities; and indirect costs such as administration. An element is included for personal living expenses. Health service costs cover hospital and community care the individual receives from outside the care home. In addition to the cost elements, the level of use of the facility and an estimate of the occupancy rate are included. Again a London multiplier is included. Weekly costs per person are given for each type of institution, and for the total care package.

A range of community care packages that support the elderly in their homes are covered in this publication[5] (Schema 1.12–1.16). To illustrate the detail included, Schema 1.14 showing a median cost community care package is shown in Table 5.1. Components included are split into social services, health services, and other; as well as accommodation and living expenses. The exact elements included vary depending on the level of support required. Social service elements could include home care, day care or respite care. Health service elements could include GP contacts, community nursing visits and chiropody. Further details on each component are given. If home care is required, the contact time is split into

Table 5.1 Unit costs for a community care package

Type of case
Mr C is 79 years old and lives with his wife in a bungalow which they jointly own. His wife is his main carer. She provides an intensive amount of assistance: changing continence pads, helping with toileting and transfers, washing soiled linen, preparing meals, shopping and other errands, liaises with formal services and monitors his medication. Mr C was recently admitted to hospital following a stroke. While there, his needs were reassessed by a social worker.

Health problems
Stroke, urinary incontinence.

Functional ability
Mr C is unable to do most activities without assistance. He has difficulty with bathing, transferring, negotiating stairs, toileting and general mobility. He needs assistance to manage his medication and money, make meals and use transport. He does no shopping, errands or heavy housework.

Services received	Average weekly cost	Description
Social services		
Home care	£68	7.25 hours per week. Visits occur Monday to Friday before 5 pm (5.75 hours per week), and on weekends (1.5 hours per week). SSD is the provider.
Health services		
Community nursing visits	£68	Two visits per week (each 45 minutes) by a district nurse.
GP	£11	Visits estimated at once every eight weeks based on GHS data.
Accommodation	£79	Based on the annuitised value of a bungalow. Taken from the Halifax Price Index, 3rd quarter 2003. Using an 8% discount rate over 60 years, the cost would be £159.
Living expenses	£161	Living expenses taken from the Family Expenditure Survey (2001/2002, uprated to 2003/2004 price levels). Based on one man one woman retired households mainly dependent on state pensions.
Total weekly cost of health and social care package, 2003/2004	£146 £386	Excludes accommodation and living expenses. Total including accommodation and living expenses.

weekday and weekend hours. Unit cost estimates for accommodation and living expenses are also given. Total weekly costs for health and social care, both inclusive and exclusive of accommodation and living expenses, are provided.

Transport

There is a short section on paramedic and emergency services (Schema 7.2).[5] Three types of service are covered: paramedic units, emergency ambulance services and patient transport services. For each service, a cost per minute and a cost per patient journey are provided.

Aids and adaptations

Unit costs for wheelchairs are given (Schema 7.3).[5] Purchase costs and annual costs for different types of wheelchair are provided. A wide range of equipment and adaptations for the home are detailed, including a concrete ramp, a stairlift, a grab rail, a hoist, additional heating, a shower and a low level bath. For each adaptation, mean and median costs are provided, and the range, as well as discounted median annual costs.

Pharmaceutical costs

Pharmaceutical costs account for 12.6% of the total costs of state-funded healthcare[6] and therefore represent an important area for the economist and decision maker. Of this spending on drugs some 79% occurs within primary care.[6] A number of sources exist for obtaining data and costs for pharmaceutical entities. These include the *British National Formulary*,[7] the *Monthly Index of Medical Specialties*[8] and the *Drug Tariff*,[9] all of which are detailed below.

British National Formulary (*BNF*)

Published jointly by the British Medical Association and the Royal Pharmaceutical Society of Great Britain, the *BNF*[7] is a comprehensive drug guide for all prescribers of medications, and is updated every six months. It is designed to be a quick reference guide for pharmaceuticals, providing up-to-date information on all medications generally used in the UK, and reflects current best practice. Although its contents do not exclusively contain drugs prescribed in primary care alone but encompass the whole spectrum of drug prescriptions (*see* Chapter 3), it is an invaluable reference source in primary care.

The book is divided into 15 systems of the body, and then into medical conditions within systems. Each section provides information to aid prescribers' selection of appropriate care, detailing the drug licence, therapeutic information, appropriate drug indications and their cautions, side effects, interactions with other drugs, and costs for each dosage given. Medications available for purchase by the general public – that is, over-the-counter medicines (OTCs) – are not covered by the *BNF*.

The *BNF* provides net costs based on costs for reimbursement for prescriptions at cost to prescribers. Costs are given for standard packs for each tablet size. This enables the cost per tablet to be calculated. Combining this information with the defined daily dose enables the cost per defined daily dose to be derived. It is this information that can be applied to any drug intervention study for the period that the drug is consumed by the patient.

As the drug tariff is set nationally, the real cost of drugs to the NHS will always be at this national rate, set by the Prescription Pricing Authority and used in the *BNF*. Where local discounts have been negotiated for a drug, these are kept or consumed by the dispenser of the drug, either the hospital trust or the local pharmacy. Although the *BNF* has a six-month lag in costs, costs reported in the *BNF* are generally adequate for use in an economic evaluation. The *BNF* is available electronically at http://www.bnf.org. There is no charge to register to view the *BNF* online.

Monthly Index of Medical Specialties (MIMS)

MIMS[8] is an alternative prescribing guide primarily used by GPs and sponsored by the pharmaceutical industry. It contains records of prescription medicines and OTC drugs. It is updated on a monthly basis and *MIMS* reflects the most up-to-date and accurate drug prices for branded drugs.

The information given includes a physical description of the drug, the manufacturer's details, and conditions the drug can be used for treating. It details situations when the drug should not be prescribed, any special precautions required or drug interactions that may occur and possible side effects. It also includes a small section on wound dressings, tapes, bandages and hosiery. Prices are included. Costs per tablet can be calculated from the prices quoted for standard packs for each tablet size. Often this price refers to the NHS price, i.e. the cost price excluding VAT (value added tax). However, some prices are marked as the retail price (including VAT) or a private prescription (excluding VAT). Again this information enables the cost per defined daily dose to be calculated and then used in any drug evaluations. As *MIMS* is produced monthly it is one of the best sources for providing alerts on new drugs coming to market. It provides summary information at the start of each issue on new products.

MIMS is sent free each month to all doctors registered with the UK General Medical Council and practising full-time in the NHS. Others can subscribe to *MIMS*, which costs £135 annually. This includes 12 copies of *MIMS* and eMIMS on CD-ROM and access to eMIMS online. eMIMS is the electronic version of *MIMS*, available at http://www.emims.net.[8]

Drug Tariff

The *Drug Tariff*[9] is produced monthly by the Prescription Pricing Authority (PPA) on behalf of the DH. The PPA's role is that of a Special Health Authority. It is responsible for calculating and making the payments to pharmacists and GPs for supplying drugs and appliances prescribed under the NHS. In addition it produces information for GPs, nurses, PCTs and other NHS stakeholders about prescribing volumes, trends and costs.

The *Drug Tariff* is freely available from the PPA website at http://www.ppa.org.uk/ppa/edt_intro.htm or http://www.drugtariff.com.[9] It gives current prices for generic drugs, appliances, dressings, chemical reagents and oxygen therapy services for the home. Each different size, for example, of dressing or drainage bag has a differential price attached. Prices are given for standard pack sizes for both drugs and dressings and this enables unit costs to be calculated easily.

The *Drug Tariff* lists drugs not to be prescribed under the NHS, and those that can be prescribed under certain conditions. It also describes circumstances in which certain food and toilet preparations should be treated and prescribed as drugs – products known as borderline substances. Nutritional supplements, such as *Fortisip* (Nutricia, Zoetermeer, The Netherlands), are one such example. These can be prescribed to patients with short bowel syndrome, pre-operatively to undernourished patients or those with disease-related malnutrition.

All three publications have their own individual merits and all overlap to some degree in the information that they provide. The *BNF* is a good starting and reference point for drug information. This can then be supplemented by the more specific information of *MIMS* and the *Drug Tariff* for proprietary and generic drugs. Citing costs from a twice-yearly publication such as the *BNF* can make it easier for readers of a study to find and adjust such costs, rather than using monthly costs from the other publications.

Screening and prevention programmes

Healthcare is not just about the treatment of conditions when they arise, but also about the early detection or prevention of conditions. Information is available on screening programmes and immunisations, and each of these is considered next.

Screening programmes

Information prepared by the Government Statistical Service on cervical and breast cancer screening programmes can be found on the DH's website. The bulletin, *Cervical Screening Programme, England: 2003–04,*[10] describes the number of women invited for screening, the number actually screened, the percentage of the target population screened of various age groups, the outcomes of smears and gynaecological referrals, and age-standardised mortality rates. Much of the information provided is broken down into age groups, regions of England, and even PCTs. Similar information on the take-up of breast cancer screening and the types of cancers detected is available in the bulletin, *Breast Screening Programme, England: 2003–04.*[11] The work of the National Screening Committee is discussed in Chapter 6.

Although we have information on the uptake of screening programmes, this information is not then linked to the efficacy of such programmes. It is not possible to tell with the information available whether the screening programme is effective. It is important to note, however, that the National Screening Committee's criterion for the implementation of a screening programme is that effective treatment is available for the condition identified. Where effective treatment is not available then the condition must be such that screening informs decision making; for example, in the case of Down's syndrome, the mother can make an informed decision surrounding termination of pregnancy or care for a child with disabilities. In terms of economic evaluation it is the combination of uptake, coverage cost and efficacy that is important. Although economics is now considered to be an integral part of screening and of the National Screening Committee's work, there are still few decisions taken on screening that truly incorporate economic information or decision making. This position is changing as screening projects are being commissioned with economic elements and there is economic input into national decision-making committees.

Given, however, the paucity of information on cost effectiveness the importance of using national data in combination with customised pieces of research work is underlined.

Immunisation statistics

Using national statistics produced by the Government Statistical Service, the bulletin, *NHS Immunisation Statistics, England: 2004–05*[12] predominantly covers the uptake of childhood immunisations, but also contains information on influenza vaccines for the over 65s. Immunisations covered include those for diphtheria, tetanus, whooping cough, measles, mumps, rubella and meningitis C. The percentages of children immunised by their first, second and fifth birthday are given. Results of tuberculin skin tests are shown together with the number of BCG vaccinations. Further information is available on reinforcing doses of diphtheria, tetanus and polio given to school leavers. Some information is broken down by region, age or provider. The information can be used when determining the likely burden of disease.

Similar information on screening and prevention programmes is available in other ONS publications such as *Social Trends* and *Regional Trends*; *see* Chapter 3 for more information. Some datasets may be available from the National Statistics website: http://www.statistics.gov.uk.

Conclusion

The disparate nature of primary care makes aggregate datasets such as the GPRD and the *Unit Costs of Health and Social Care* particularly useful for people involved in primary care research. Such data sources allow access to a large amount of data without the need to contact individual practitioners to obtain such data. The data provided at an aggregate level may then be applied to local studies where minimum data may have been gathered but not full economic data. Similarly in areas such as pharmaceutical prices at a primary care level, each individual practitioner is subject to the national price structure. This chapter has emphasised the role of aggregate datasets to supplement local information or, in the absence of local information, the usefulness of such datasets.

References

1 General Practice Research Database: http://www.gprd.com.
2 Walley T and Mantgani A (1997) The UK General Practice Research Database. *The Lancet*. **350**: 1097–9.
3 Medicines and Healthcare products Regulatory Agency: http://www.mhra.gov.uk.
4 Office for National Statistics (ONS) (1998) *Key Health Statistics from General Practice*. ONS, London. Also available at http://www.statistics.gov.uk/products/p4863.asp.
5 Curtis L and Netten A (2004) *Unit Costs of Health and Social Care 2004*. PSSRU, University of Kent, Canterbury. Also available at http://www.pssru.ac.uk/uc/uc2004.htm.
6 Office of Health Economics (OHE) (2003) *OHE Compendium of Health Statistics* (15e). Section 4, Family Health Services, Table 4.58. OHE, London.
7 British Medical Association and the Royal Pharmaceutical Society of Great Britain (2005) *British National Formulary*. **50**. British Medical Association and The Pharmaceutical Press, London. Also available at http://www.bnf.org.
8 *Monthly Index of Medical Specialties (MIMS)* (2005). August. Haymarket Medical, London. Also available at http://www.emims.net.
9 Department of Health (2005) *Drug Tariff*. November. The Stationery Office, London. Also available at http://www.ppa.org.uk/ppa/edt_intro.htm or http://www.drugtariff.com.
10 Department of Health (2004) *Cervical Screening Programme, England: 2003–04*. Statistical Bulletin 2004/20. Available from http://www.dh.gov.uk, follow links for Publications and statistics, Statistics, Statistical work areas, Statistical work areas: health care, Screening and immunisation.
11 Department of Health (2005) *Breast Screening Programme, England: 2003–04*. Statistical Bulletin 2005/06. Available from http://www.dh.gov.uk, follow links for Publications and statistics, Statistics, Statistical work areas, Statistical work areas: health care, Screening and immunisation.
12 Health and Social Care Information Centre (2005) *NHS Immunisation Statistics, England: 2004–05*. Statistical Bulletin 2005/05/HSCIC. Available from http://www.dh.gov.uk, follow links for Publications and statistics, Statistics, Statistical work areas, Statistical work areas: health care, Screening and immunisation.

6 Organisations providing health economic information

Introduction

The aim of this chapter is to introduce the reader to organisations that produce health economic information. This will familiarise the reader with what specific institutions have available, rather than defining the location of any one piece of information. This chapter is about starting broad and then honing in on specific information. It is concerned with the availability and application of secondary data sources rather than primary data gathering. Unlike Chapters 4 and 5 that just consider secondary and primary care data alone, this chapter will present broad categories of national aggregate data. It will show that health economic data is not only found in organisations solely concerned with health but also in related areas. In keeping with the rest of this book, information will be discussed and presented for its contribution to economic understanding and ultimately decision making.

The chapter will seek to introduce the reader to the full range of organisations that provide data useful for health economics: their function, the type of data provided, and the potential use and application of such data. The data required for health economic evaluations come from many sources. The organisations reviewed represent the most important sources of information. Not surprisingly the main organisation providing data used for an economic evaluation is the Department of Health and its associated bodies such as the National Institute for Health and Clinical Excellence. It is important to note, however, that other government bodies such as the Office for National Statistics and the Department for Work and Pensions, and non-governmental organisations such as the Office of Health Economics, also provide information that may be valuable in economic terms. Finally, global data as provided by the World Health Organization are described.

Department of Health (DH)

As the most important source of information for health economists, the DH can provide information on public health, social care, healthcare, workforce and expenditure. Public health information covers indicators of the nation's health (death rates, cases of infectious diseases); smoking, drinking and drug use; and fertility and maternity. Further information on birth and maternity statistics can be found in *Harnessing Official Statistics*.[1] Healthcare information includes hospital activity (*see* Chapter 3), community care, mental health, ophthalmics and dentistry, as well as screening and prevention programmes. Further information can be found from the DH website, http://www.dh.gov.uk,[2] and links to these topics can be found by selecting Publications and statistics, Statistics, and Statistical work areas.

The DH can produce information ranging from screening activities (*see* Chapter 5) to treatment evaluations. They also produce costing information, and NHS Reference Costs are described in Chapter 3. Part of the DH's role is to disseminate information on best practice and to set national standards. This is the aim of National Service Frameworks, which are described below (and also the aim of the NHS organisation the National Institute for Health and Clinical Excellence, described later). To assist in identifying best practice, the DH funds a national programme of research, the Health Technology Assessment programme, which is also described below.

National Service Frameworks (NSFs)

NSFs detail how services can best be provided to patients with particular conditions, and set national standards for the provision of that care. They also set milestones for the improvement of services, and are one of the initiatives to raise standards of care and reduce variations across the country. NSFs have been produced in areas such as elderly care, mental health, diabetes, children's services, and long-term conditions – with a focus on neurological conditions. Details of NSFs can be found from the DH website,[2] then follow links for Policy and guidance, Health and social care topics, and National Service Frameworks.

NSFs focus on major health issues. Coronary heart disease (CHD), as one of the most common causes of fatalities, is high on this agenda. In 2000, the NSF for CHD was launched.[3] It notes that although there is a wealth of evidence for prevention, diagnosis and treatment of CHD, this knowledge is applied unsystematically. The NSF sets 12 standards covering all aspects of CHD: for example reducing the prevalence of heart disease, preventative measures for those at high risk of CHD, standards for the speed of delivering care to those suffering a heart attack, and investigations that should be available to those suspected of suffering heart failure. Milestones are also set for specific rapid improvements as well as longer-term aims. NSFs set economic targets, and hence become important for economic evaluations.

Although the NSFs are not primarily designed to address health economic issues, the substance upon which they are based has certain implications for the use and distribution of costs as they relate to effectiveness. The NSFs address healthcare goals, treatments and good practice guidelines for whole populations. The challenge for health economics is to take these guidelines and apply them within the envelope of available resources. Some of the NSFs, for example the NSF on diabetes,[4] have specific recommendations based on the underlying economic evidence. (*See* sections 3.6 and 3.7 NSF for Diabetes,[4] which draws upon a fuller report of the National Screening Committee, *Preservation of Sight in Diabetes: a risk reduction programme*.[5]) Hence the NSF could have links to important economic evidence or may have suggested links to other sites that contain specific economic information.

Health Technology Assessment (HTA) programme

The HTA programme is a national programme of research. Health technology covers a broad spectrum of methods for the prevention, diagnosis or treatment of disease, and improvements in rehabilitation or palliative care. The HTA programme aims to produce high quality research on the clinical and cost effectiveness of health technologies to inform decision makers within the NHS. It is funded by the DH's Research and Development programme.

The HTA programme receives many suggestions of technologies to appraise from within the NHS, patients, and organisations such as the National Institute for Health and Clinical Excellence (NICE). It is necessary to identify where knowledge is lacking and then to prioritise research according to factors such as the topic's importance, and the level of uncertainty around the technology. Once a topic is identified as a priority, research is commissioned and monitored by the HTA programme. After the final report has been peer-reviewed and accepted, it is published as an HTA monograph. These are freely available to download from the web at http://www.hta.nhsweb.nhs.uk.

Through this process, the HTA programme supports the work of NICE. NICE provides appraisals of technologies and produces guidance on best practice. Once NICE has identified the technologies it wishes to appraise, the HTA programme commissions an assessment report. Once this has been submitted to NICE, and NICE have published their guidance, the assessment reports are published in the HTA monograph series. The work of NICE is described next, and in the technology appraisal section that follows is an example of the HTA programme supporting the work of NICE.

National Institute for Health and Clinical Excellence (NICE)

In April 1999, the National Institute for Clinical Excellence was set up as a special health authority for England and Wales. Its role is to provide clear guidance to health professionals, patients and the public on current best clinical practice, and the effectiveness of new treatments, based on reliable evidence. In this way, NICE supports the implementation of NSFs. In April 2005, it took on the functions of the Health Development Agency, and became the National Institute for Health and Clinical Excellence (NICE). Further information about NICE can be found at http://www.nice.org.uk.

Incorporated into NICE is a very specific focus upon health economics and health economic information. NICE base their decisions not only on clinical efficacy but also on the cost effectiveness argument. A hypothetical although unreferenced threshold of £30 000 per Quality Adjusted Life Year (QALY), *see* Chapter 7, is often quoted as a criterion for a therapy to receive NICE approval.[6] NICE draws upon health economic information provided within the HTA reports and elsewhere and issues NICE guidance that has a clear economic focus. The information from which NICE makes its decisions, whether commissioned or provided by independent companies or academic institutions, includes economic information. Information reviewed may take many different forms including randomised controlled trials (RCTs), economic models and company data on file. NICE addresses the expected costs of an intervention, quality of life issues including QALYs and discounting.

NICE technology appraisals and guidance are closely related but result in separate reports for technology appraisals, clinical guidelines and interventional procedures. The emphasis on including economic evidence in submissions to NICE ensures that the reports take into account not only clinical evidence but also economic evidence. In terms of economics it is the technology appraisal reports that provide economic data in a readily accessible form for economic decision making. The clinical and interventional guideline reports provide clinical information informed by economic thinking. They are written in clear language that can be accessed by any decision maker, consumer of care, technical expert or non-specialist manager. The requirement to include economic evidence has increased the number of economic studies undertaken and published by companies, and as such has helped to contribute to the increased availability of economic information. The technology assessment appraisals specifically are discussed in the next section.

Technology appraisals

NICE provides clinical and cost effectiveness appraisals of new and existing technologies (products such as medicines, devices and surgical procedures), and produces clinical guidelines for the treatment of specific conditions. More information on technologies can be found in the section on the Health Technology Assessment Database later in this chapter. The case to support an intervention is made by the company producing the product, supported by clinical and economic data. NICE requires information on costs and benefits, and where possible QALYs. Where QALY information is not available from RCTs, NICE will accept the use of modelling evidence upon which to make decisions regarding the use of medical interventions. The evidence is independently reviewed by an expert panel. Audit methodologies are provided to support the appraisals and guidelines. Guidance is then issued regarding the use of the intervention. A decision is made both on efficacy and cost effectiveness grounds. By focusing on the most cost effective, the NHS will make best use of available resources. This should promote a better, efficient and more uniform level of care across the country. It should be noted that although NICE guidance is there to support decision makers, it is not currently mandatory to follow such guidance. Information on completed technology appraisals can be found by selecting Clinical Excellence, Our guidance, Technology appraisals and then Published appraisals from http://www.nice.org.uk.

Clinical and trial data often make a clear case for the safety and efficacy of a product, but NICE considers the cost efficacy of such interventions compared against their competitors, often drawing heavily on the evidence from HTA programme reports (as described in the previous section). The reports produced by the HTA programme allow such issues to be explored. They present cost structures for an intervention that can be compared with the benefits yielded. By using these as a starting point, sensitivity analyses and economic models can then be presented for a range of scenarios, thus making the economic case for an intervention from these assumptions and scenarios using the best evidence available.

An example of the approach and issues is the following NICE appraisal on the use of riluzole for the treatment of motor neurone disease (MND).[7] Riluzole can extend the time before mechanical assistance is required with breathing, and extend life. The appraisal recommended riluzole for patients with a particular form of motor neurone disease, amyotrophic lateral sclerosis (ALS), and the treatment should be initiated by a neurological specialist with experience in treating MND.

The appraisal guidance[7] is based on research that considers the efficacy and cost effectiveness of riluzole. It brings together evidence from the manufacturer and independent evidence; and takes into account an assessment report,[8] the manufacturer's submission and the views of specialist and professional groups. The results from four RCTs were considered, and combined where appropriate. Many uncertainties surround the cost effectiveness estimates available. The manufacturer's estimates, and estimates based on more conservative outcome probabilities, were considered. The more conservative discounted cost per QALY estimates were in the region of £34 000 to £43 500. Given the relatively short lifespan of patients with ALS and the value they place on extending the time until mechanical ventilation is required, the appraisal committee considered the cost implications to the NHS were outweighed by the benefit to these patients. Hence riluzole is recommended for patients with ALS. This provides a further example of economic input being used to inform decision making.

The guidance from appraisals can be either used to inform readers when undertaking their own appraisals or used to inform decision making in the absence of local evidence.

UK National Screening Committee (NSC)

The NSC[9] was set up under the auspices of the DH, but as a separate body, to advise on the evaluation and implementation of screening programmes.[10] The documents produced and reviewed by the NSC cover all aspects of screening from the clinical to the economic. Screening identifies those who are at risk of having a disease or its complications, such that they may be offered further tests or treatment to reduce the risk of a disease or its complications. More information on specific screening programmes (cervical and breast cancer) can be found in Chapter 5.

The NSC advises ministers across the four countries of the UK on all aspects of screening policy, and in particular antenatal and child health screening policies. The NSC uses all the available research evidence, as well as multidisciplinary expert groups, in order to make its decisions. Members of the groups include public health representatives, consultants, specialist scientists, health economists and patient representatives.

New proposals for screening programmes are assessed against the NSC criteria. The NSC ensures that new programmes will provide a benefit to the population, and crucially are cost effective. Decision makers may find it as helpful to consider what is excluded from the NSC's recommendations as to what is included. Many types of screening become common practice without either sufficient supporting evidence being available as to their benefit, or even in the face of contrary evidence in terms of patient benefit; as such they are an unnecessary drain on healthcare resources. The NHS cannot introduce any new screening programmes until the NSC has reviewed their effectiveness and made subsequent recommendations.[9]

The NSC is not a research organisation but will always review any new test or recommendation for its health economic implications. It will from time to time commission or produce specific technical health economic reports, for example the cost effectiveness model for diabetic retinopathy,[11] or short technical heath economic recommendations.

Office for National Statistics (ONS)

ONS is the government agency that provides economic and social statistics for England and Wales. It also has responsibility for the Census, and for the registration of all births, deaths and marriages in England and Wales. ONS was formed in April 1996, after the merger of the Central Statistical Office and the Office for Population Censuses and Surveys (OPCS).

The ONS website, http://www.statistics.gov.uk, provides detailed information on government statistics and publications. The data produced by ONS are varied and can serve many purposes. Information is divided into themes, of which health and care is the most relevant for this book. This theme is subdivided into care, quality of life, and health. Vast amounts of information are available on a range of topics and in great detail. One topic covered within health is deaths, which includes mortality rates, causes of deaths, childhood deaths, and coding of deaths. Other topics within health are abortions, child health, accidents and injuries, and morbidities such as cancer, coronary heart disease, and asthma. Within each topic, datasets and publications are listed.

Chapter 3 covers ONS data on mortality statistics, life expectancy and cancer registrations. A range of surveys that ONS are involved in – including the Census, *Social Trends* and the General Household Survey – is also covered in Chapter 3. Vaccination statistics and screening programmes are covered in Chapter 5. More information on ONS data, in particular birth and mortality statistics, and cancer registries, can be found in *Harnessing Official Statistics*.[12]

Broadly aggregated data may be used and applied in local studies. A study may for example be too small in its own right to indicate a true mortality rate in the study population, hence the use of ONS data (*see* Chapter 3). The analyst may wish to undertake analysis based on scenarios and figures obtained from the national dataset. In contrast to the broad aggregate data, utilisation of the Census data may enable the analyst to apply very specific local estimates to the calculation of any effects on costs and benefits from an intervention.

Department for Work and Pensions (DWP)

The DWP[13] is responsible for jobs and benefits, and aims to promote independence for everyone. It provides support and advice to the whole spectrum of the population – those of working age, children, pensioners, disabled people and employers. The DWP produces the Abstract of Statistics, in which the Average Earnings Index is of primary interest. This is described next.

Abstract of Statistics

The Abstract of Statistics[14] summarises information on the main benefits, contributions and indices of prices and earnings. The Information Directorate of the DWP publishes it annually. The Abstract of Statistics is available from http://www.dwp.gov.uk/asd/asd1/abstract/Abstract2004.pdf.[14]

Although many studies only focus upon the direct costs of care, often to the health sector, a number of studies seek to address the broader societal effects of an intervention. These studies may not only look to measure the direct costs of care, but the indirect costs of care – that is, the effect on a person's employment or use of their time because of a healthcare intervention. The Abstract of Statistics shows the average earnings by OPCS social class classification, and for men and women and all groups combined, year on year. These figures can be used as a proxy for the calculation of indirect costs within an economic evaluation – that is, time lost from paid employment due to a healthcare intervention or illness. Although there are many potential problems in using such figures as a proxy for time lost due to illness (for example, how to impute values for the unemployed, retired or carers) it is less contentious to use such figures than ask people about their actual earnings. A further issue to consider is whether to allow for time off work being frictional – that is, subsumed by the employer and covered by social insurance schemes such as statutory sick pay.

Cochrane Collaboration

The Cochrane Collaboration was set up in 1993 to help people make informed healthcare decisions by providing up-to-date systematic reviews of healthcare interventions. This is important because although results from individual trials may prove inconclusive, by combining the results from similar trials, a more robust conclusion may be reached. By preparing and maintaining systematic reviews, the Cochrane Collaboration aims to provide up-to-date and accessible evidence, avoid the duplication of work, and allow new research to be targeted efficiently. The Cochrane Collaboration also reviews the methodology of systematic reviews, ensuring high standards. More information on the Cochrane Collaboration can be found at http://www.cochrane.org. The different elements of the Cochrane Collaboration will be discussed below.

Cochrane Library

The Cochrane Library is a collection of evidence-based medical databases available from http://www3.interscience.wiley.com/cgi-bin/mrwhome/106568753/HOME, and is published quarterly. The Cochrane Database of Systematic Reviews (discussed below) is part of the Cochrane Library. Other databases included in the Cochrane Library are the Cochrane Controlled Trials Register, Database of Abstracts of Reviews of Effects (DARE), Cochrane Methodology Register, NHS Economic Evaluation Database (NHS EED), Health Technology Assessment (HTA) Database, and Cochrane Database of Methodology Reviews (CDMR). The Cochrane Controlled Trials Register contains bibliographical information on thousands of controlled trials, including those published in conference proceedings and other sources not generally included in bibliographical databases. Further information on DARE, NHS EED, and the HTA Database can be found in the next section on the NHS Centre for Reviews and Dissemination.

The information provided by the Cochrane Library is useful for framing future evaluations. Cochrane reviews include economic information. Such information can help identify important cost drivers and key outcomes. These are important in the subsequent design of new trials and in the identification of key parameters for economic modelling. Similarly, economic methods themselves have formed the basis for a Cochrane review. Again, these provide important information from which to undertake new research. They can help guide the analyst towards the most appropriate method for any new work.

The Cochrane Library is freely accessible in several countries (including England, Wales and Ireland). Information on accessing the Cochrane Library by subscription or national provision in these and other countries is available from http://www3.interscience.wiley.com/cgi-bin/mrwhome/106568753/HOME. In England, the National electronic Library for Health provides funds, allowing residents of England to access the Cochrane Library at http://www.nelh.nhs.uk/cochrane.asp.

Cochrane Database of Systematic Reviews

The key publications from the Cochrane Collaboration are the Cochrane reviews, published in the Cochrane Database of Systematic Reviews. Each review contains information on its methodology, the results including statistical pooling of results (meta-analysis) and a discussion of the results and their implications for practice. Information on the methodological quality of each study is given, as well as full references of all studies included, and for studies excluded (with reasons for their exclusion). The Cochrane Database of Systematic Reviews can be found in the Cochrane Library, which is published quarterly. Reviews may be updated with new evidence or errors amended in successive publications. Structured abstracts of the reviews can be obtained free of charge.[15]

Cochrane systematic reviews are a useful source of additional information. One way such information may be used is in providing detail on economic variables that could not be collected in the study. Further as Cochrane reviews take their evidence from a number of studies they enable information to be pooled from a larger study set than a single study itself. The results of this pooled analysis may show less variability than a single study result. They may be used in conjunction with an actual study to provide the basis for a sensitivity analysis, or for future modelling studies. Although economic data are now included in the database, many of the reviews have only a clinical focus, hence for the economic analyst it is still much easier to find additional information on clinical factors rather than economic factors.

NHS Centre for Reviews and Dissemination (CRD)

Established in 1994 and based in York, the NHS Centre for Reviews and Dissemination aims to promote research-based practice by disseminating information on the effectiveness of treatments to NHS decision makers and healthcare professionals. The NHS Executive and the Health Departments of Wales and Northern Ireland fund it. Further information can be found at http://www.york.ac.uk/inst/crd/.

The CRD manages three databases: the Health Technology Assessment (HTA) Database; the Database of Abstracts of Reviews of Effects (DARE); and the NHS Economic Evaluation Database (NHS EED). These databases are freely accessible from the CRD website. Each database will now be considered.

Health Technology Assessment (HTA) Database

This database contains records of ongoing research into healthcare technologies. Healthcare technologies range from medicines, vaccines, medical devices and diagnostic techniques to medical and surgical procedures. Assessment of these technologies is made from a very broad perspective covering the medical, ethical, economic and social implications. The aim is to improve the clinical effectiveness and cost effectiveness of such technologies and to inform policy. The HTA Database can be accessed free of charge at http://www.york.ac.uk/inst/crd/htahp.htm, or through the Cochrane Library.

Since records in the HTA Database come from several sources, there are variations in the amount of information included in each abstract. Every record gives a title, type and year of publication and an address for correspondence. Many detail the authors' objective, the type of intervention, the study design and authors' conclusions. Where a systematic review has been performed, details of the sources searched are given, and the results of the review may be available. If any cost information is reported, this will be indicated in the record. The database is produced with assistance from the International Network of Agencies for Health Technology Assessments (INAHTA). This body aims to promote the sharing of information between those who assess health technologies. It provides the CRD with records of ongoing work and publications in healthcare technology assessment every six months.

Database of Abstracts of Reviews of Effects (DARE)

DARE was created in 1995 by the CRD, and is updated monthly. It contains abstracts of systematic reviews on a broad range of healthcare technologies. DARE can be accessed free of charge at http://www.york.ac.uk/inst/crd/darehp.htm, or through the Cochrane Library.[15] It aims to identify systematic reviews that are of a high methodological standard. Potential reviews are identified by searching major medical journals, bibliographical databases and grey literature. Reviews must consider the effectiveness or side effects of at least one intervention or method for organising healthcare. The reviews will have a clearly defined question, and provide evidence of a wide literature search. The quality of individual studies will have been taken into account. A description of the overall picture from the individual studies will be reported, and where possible the results will be combined quantitatively, by meta-analysis. The importance to health economics lies in the provision of effectiveness data for use in modelling and to inform the design of evaluations.

Each abstract provides comprehensive information on the methodology, including the objective, the intervention, patient inclusion criteria, the primary outcome used, the sources searched, details of how data were extracted from studies, how they were combined, and how any differences between studies were investigated. Details are given of the number of studies included, results and conclusions. A commentary written by a CRD reviewer is also included, which discusses the methodological strengths and weaknesses of the review. There are currently over 2200 detailed abstracts in DARE.

As methods for systematic reviewing have advanced, the standards of the reviews included in DARE have risen too. The reviews were all of a high quality at the time they were produced. However, it is important to note that earlier reviews would now not be considered to follow the current pre-defined standards.

NHS Economic Evaluation Database (NHS EED)

Funded by the DH, the NHS EED is managed by the CRD. (It should not be confused with the Health Economic Evaluations Database (HEED) described later.) NHS EED contains summaries and assessments of economic evaluations, identified from vast quantities of literature. It is a time-saving and useful tool for decision makers and researchers and a good starting point for a literature search. The types of economic evaluation included are cost minimisation, cost benefit, cost consequences, cost effectiveness and cost utility analyses. Potential studies are found by searching major medical journals and bibliographical databases. The working papers from research centres specialising in technology assessments or health economics are also scanned. There are many checks in place to ensure that information in NHS EED is accurate and of high quality.

Full economic evaluations have an abstract on the database, which summarises and assesses the evaluation. Bibliographical details only are included for papers on methodology, cost of treatment, policy, or partial evaluations. Also included in NHS EED are revised abstracts from the Register of Cost Effectiveness Studies records. The NHS EED is freely available at http://www.york.ac.uk/inst/crd/nhsdhp.htm and is updated monthly. NHS EED can also be accessed through the Cochrane Library,[15] where it is updated quarterly. Work began on NHS EED in February 1995, so studies published before then do not appear on the database.

NHS EED can be searched by type of record, i.e. economic evaluation or costing/methodology study, as well as by author, title, date of publication and by subject headings. Each full abstract details the health technology being assessed and the disease group to which it relates. Basic information such as the study question, the type of economic evaluation, the study design, population and setting are recorded. More details of the economic analysis are also given. In the case of benefit, the measure used is recorded and the method of analysis. The direct costs included are reported. Cost and benefit results are reported separately and are then combined. Where the abstract reports a review of previously published literature, the inclusion criteria for the review, the sources of primary studies, and the methods used to combine them are given. Details are given of any sensitivity analyses performed, if applicable. Finally the authors' conclusions are given, along with the CRD reviewer's commentary and the implications of the study.

Office of Health Economics (OHE)

Founded in 1962, the OHE undertakes research into the economics of health and healthcare, and analyses data from around the world. More information is available from the OHE website at http://www.ohe.org. Publications from the OHE are considered in the next sections.

OHE Compendium of Health Statistics

Published in 2005, the 17th edition[16] provides detailed information on health and healthcare and their costs in the UK. It draws comparisons over time, and with other developed countries. Information is provided at a regional as well as a national level, where possible. The Compendium covers four broad areas. The first looks at UK demographic details and mortality and morbidity statistics. The second section examines the cost of the NHS and expenditure on healthcare. Thirdly, it provides information on NHS hospital activity, bed capacity and the workforce. The final section covers NHS family health services including general medical, pharmaceutical, dental and ophthalmic services. The book and CD-ROM of the Compendium can be obtained from the OHE for a fee; current prices and further information are available from the Compendium's website at http://www.ohecompendium.org.

Of particular interest to health economists is the detailed coverage of Reference Costs in Section 3. For example, Reference Costs for the top 40 Healthcare Resource Groups (HRGs) ranked by total cost are provided for elective and non-elective inpatients. (For further details on Reference Costs *see* Chapter 3; for HRGs *see* Chapter 4.)

OHE publications

The OHE produces discussion papers and books. Topics range from specific disease areas, to methodological issues in economic evaluations to broader issues in the provision of healthcare. One of interest is on cost effectiveness thresholds.[17] This discusses whether NICE should have a threshold of cost effectiveness and whether this should be explicit. It covers the use of thresholds, and ethical considerations. NICE responds to the suggestion that it has a threshold of £30 000 per QALY – a view held by some based on past decisions made by NICE. Public involvement in decision making is discussed, as are ways forward.

OHE Health Economic Evaluations Database (HEED)

HEED is a joint initiative between the OHE and the International Federation of Pharmaceutical Manufacturers' Associations (IFPMA). It should not be confused with NHS EED, which is a separate database (described earlier). HEED contains more than 31 500 references (as of August 2005) relating to the economic assessment of healthcare technologies. Entries in the database are either bibliographic references or references which have been reviewed by a health economist, and the information contained within the paper abstracted out into a readily accessible form. Nearly half the references in the database have been reviewed and are useful to health economists as they cover both costs and benefits of an intervention. Some information on HEED can be found from the main OHE website; however, there is a specific HEED website at http://www.ohe-heed.com from which a demonstration site can be accessed. Access is however expensive: the annual subscription is over £1000 for non-profit-making organisations. Further information is available from the HEED website.

New references are added to HEED monthly. These are identified by database searches, hand searches of a number of medical, health economic and policy journals and by review of publications from a selection of academic and government centres. Specific details can be found from the HEED website. HEED comprehensively covers the period from 1992 onwards, although there are some older references included in the database. The key features of the economic evaluation literature covered by HEED are described in the OHE briefing, *Trends in Economic Evaluation*.[18]

The reviewed articles are categorised into different groups. The three main ones are applied studies (by far the largest group), reviews of applied studies and methodological studies. Reviewed articles are also categorised by the type of economic evaluation. These include the main types: cost minimisation, cost benefit, cost consequences, cost effectiveness, and cost utility analyses as well as cost of illness and costing studies that compare the relative costs of two or more interventions for a condition. Searches of HEED can be made not only by type of article, and by type of evaluation, but also by author, journal, publication status (for example, book, peer-reviewed journal), technology assessed, drug name, International Classification of Diseases (ICD) codes and by keywords.

Within each reviewed article, basic information such as the date of publication, full reference and intervention is supplemented with more detailed economic information. Details of the sources of quantities of resource used within the intervention, and of resource costs, are given, as well as the types of costs included and the base year for costings. The type of outcome measures used within the study is recorded. The study question, patient characteristics and key results are also given. Further information is given regarding any discounting and sensitivity analysis performed.

Chartered Institute of Public Finance and Accountancy (CIPFA)

CIPFA is a professional accountancy body in the UK that specialises in the public services. It provides qualifications and further training for professional accountants, courses, publications and consultancy services, both in the UK and internationally. CIPFA is responsible for local government accounting standards. Much more information about CIPFA can be found at http://www.cipfa.org.uk. It is their publication, the Health Service Financial Database, that is of interest to health economists, and is described next.

Health Service Financial Database

Published by the Institute of Public Finance, the commercial arm of CIPFA, the Health Service Financial Database[19] provides financial information on all NHS trusts, Primary Care Trusts (PCTs) and Strategic Health Authorities in England and Wales. Information is taken from the statutory trust and Strategic Health Authority annual accounts and financial returns. Further information is included on hospital waiting times and NHS performance star ratings. This database includes specialty costs per inpatient day, inpatient episode, and outpatient attendance and information on length of stay by trust and by PCT. The data provided are useful as they present an average specialty cost that may be applied broadly across different hospital wards for differing interventions. Data may be available on length of stay within a study, but the actual cost incurred during a hospital stay may not be easy to collect. The Health Service Financial Database can provide data that enable average specialty costs to be applied to a hospital stay.

World Health Organization (WHO)

The WHO was formed in 1948 in order to help people around the world achieve their best possible health state. The WHO definition for health is 'a state of complete physical, mental and social well-being and not merely the absence of disease or infirmity'. The WHO aims to reduce mortality and morbidity, promote healthy lifestyles and develop healthcare systems that are equitable. More information on the WHO can be found on their website: http://www.who.int.

Each year the WHO produces the *World Health Report*, focusing on a particular theme. The report looks at the situation across the world, reviews the current burden of a disease/condition, and indicates where health gains can be made. Recommendations are made that can be implemented to a greater or lesser extent by all countries. Two of the recent reports are discussed in more detail next.

The *World Health Report 2003*[20] focused on the importance of health systems. The current state of world health is described, including the large gap in life expectancy between the poorest developing countries and elsewhere. The Millennium Development Goals are described, as is the progress so far towards achieving them. Three diseases are described in detail: HIV/AIDS (human immunodeficiency disease/acquired immune deficiency disease), polio, and SARS (severe acute respiratory syndrome). The chapter devoted to HIV/AIDS describes the trends in the HIV epidemic, the successes and failures to date in tackling the disease, and the goals for the future. The success so far of the campaign to eradicate polio is described, which highlights the need for partnerships; however, considerable obstacles remain. The rapid containment of the SARS outbreak is one of the public health successes in recent years, and the lessons learnt from the epidemic are detailed. Other growing epidemics of non-communicable diseases and injuries are discussed – in particular, cardiovascular disease, tobacco-related illnesses, and the many hazards associated with an increase in road traffic. A key message of this report is that in order to improve health and reduce health inequalities, healthcare systems need to be strengthened and based on primary care. Systems must also balance health promotion and disease prevention with treatment for acute and chronic conditions.

The 2005 report is subtitled *Make every mother and child count.*[21] The report highlights high levels of maternal and childhood deaths. Many of these deaths are avoidable, and worryingly the situation has worsened in some countries in recent years. Reducing these deaths is in line with the Millennium Development Goals, one of which aims to reduce child mortality and another aims to improve maternal health. The report calls for continuity of care through pregnancy, childbirth and into childhood. There is a particular need to strengthen healthcare available to newborns. Health systems will need to be strengthened in order to achieve these aims, and significant investment is required. It is imperative that the health workforce needed for improving these services is put in place; this will be the focus of the *World Health Report 2006.*

Global Burden of Disease (GBD)

Studies to measure the Global Burden of Disease are regularly produced by the WHO. Such studies are important when comparing need across countries and continents. One of the key indicators of health outcome developed by the World Bank, and a key tool used in such studies, is the Disability Adjusted Life Year (DALY), which was introduced in 1993. It represents the present value of future years of life lost from a disease, adjusted for age, disability and future time. A DALY, for example, would weight more highly the life of a 40 year old compared to a five year old. This reflects the weight attached to each age state, which relates to typical social role at each age. Hence a year lived at age 40 is considered more important than a year lived at age five.

It is desirable to have a measure of health status that takes morbidity as well as mortality into account. The DALY represents a measure of health status that allows morbidity and mortality to be addressed on a global scale.[22] DALYs score health status on a severity scale of 0 to 1, where 0 represents no problems, and 1 represents death or a health state equivalent to death. The DALY can be used as a practical tool to target resources to those conditions where need is greatest as measured by total health loss.

Conclusion

The chapter has reviewed some of the main organisations that provide health economic information. It has outlined the types and uses of the information they hold in terms of their value to health economic decision making and appraisals, in the past, currently, and in the future. In addition it has shown the databases that exist that hold specific health economic information.

References

1 Macfarlane A (2000) Birth and maternity statistics. In: D Leadbeter (ed.) *Harnessing Official Statistics*. Harnessing Health Information Series. Radcliffe Medical Press, Oxford.
2 Department of Health: http://www.dh.gov.uk.
3 Department of Health (DH) (2000) *National Service Framework for Coronary Heart Disease: modern standards and service models*. DH, London.
4 Department of Health (DH) (2002) *National Service Framework for Diabetes: modern standards and service models*. DH, London.
5 National Screening Committee (2000) *Preservation of Sight in Diabetes: a risk reduction programme*. Available at http://www.nsc.nhs.uk/pdfs/secondreport.pdf.
6 Towse A and Pritchard C (2002) Does NICE have a threshold? An

external view. In: A Towse, C Pritchard and N Devlin (eds) *Cost-effectiveness Thresholds: economic and ethical issues.* King's Fund and Office of Health Economics, London.

7 National Institute for Clinical Excellence (2000) *Guidance on the Use of Riluzole (Rilutek) for the Treatment of Motor Neurone Disease.* Available from http://www.nice.org.uk, then select Clinical Excellence, Our guidance, Technology appraisals, Published appraisals.

8 Stewart A, Sandercock J, Bryan S *et al.* (2000) *The Clinical Effectiveness and Cost-effectiveness of Riluzole for Motor Neurone Disease.* Submission to NICE. Available from http://www.nice.org.uk, then select Clinical Excellence, Our guidance, Technology appraisals, Published appraisals.

9 National Screening Committee: http://www.nsc.nhs.uk/.

10 NHS Executive (1996) *Improving the Effectiveness of Clinical Services.* Executive Letter EL(96)110. NHSE, Leeds.

11 James M and Little R (2001) *Screening for Diabetic Retinopathy. Report to the National Screening Committee.* Available from Centre for Health Planning and Management, Keele University, Keele, Staffordshire.

12 Leadbeter D (ed.) (2000) *Harnessing Official Statistics.* Harnessing Health Information Series. Radcliffe Medical Press, Oxford.

13 Department for Work and Pensions: http://www.dwp.gov.uk.

14 Department for Work and Pensions (2005) *The Abstract of Statistics for Benefits, Contributions and Indices of Prices and Earnings: 2004 Edition.* DWP, London. Available at http://www.dwp.gov.uk/asd/asd1/abstract/Abstract2004.pdf.

15 The Cochrane Library: http://www3.interscience.wiley.com/cgi-bin/mrwhome/106568753/HOME.

16 Yuen P (2005) *OHE Compendium of Health Statistics* (17e). Office of Health Economics, London.

17 Towse A, Pritchard C and Devlin N (eds) (2002) *Cost-effectiveness Thresholds: economic and ethical issues.* King's Fund and Office of Health Economics, London.

18 Pritchard C (1998) *Trends in Economic Evaluation.* OHE Briefing No. 36. Office of Health Economics, London.

19 Institute of Public Finance (IPF) (2003) *Health Service Financial Database.* IPF, London.

20 World Health Organization (2003) *World Health Report 2003. Shaping the future.* WHO, Geneva.

21 World Health Organization (2005) *World Health Report 2005. Make every mother and child count.* WHO, Geneva.

22 Murray CJL and Lopez AD (1994) Quantifying disability: data, methods and results. In: CJL Murray and AD Lopez (eds) *Global Comparative Assessment in the Health Sector: disease burden, expenditures and interventions.* World Health Organization, Geneva, pp. 55–96.

7 Measuring benefits and preferences

Introduction

Health economics focuses upon the measurement of costs and benefits. Without considering fully both sides of the equation, there is no economic argument. In terms of economics and efficiency in general, as we have demonstrated in Chapter 1, it is the measurement of both costs and benefits in combination that is important in achieving efficiency. It is not merely appropriate to maximise benefits or minimise cost in isolation from the other. This chapter focuses on the different techniques and measurement instruments available for determining benefit in economic appraisals. The following chapter will focus upon measuring resource use.

Benefit is an improvement in any form of health status. This includes functional benefit, which is an improvement in the ability to perform usual activities such as household tasks and walking. Benefit not only encompasses the ability to perform everyday tasks but also includes complete holistic, mental and physical well-being. In some instances, a beneficial outcome may be maintaining the pre-intervention level of health status, or a swift return to pre-intervention levels. The health status of surgical patients may not improve immediately, and initially may decline, but then improve to greater than the pre-surgical state.

Unless some form of outcome or benefit is measured, it is impossible to determine if one treatment is in some sense 'better' than another. Minimising cost alone is insufficient; it is always possible to minimise cost. Health economists are concerned with costs and benefits. To look at costs alone would be nonsensical. It is necessary to show that a treatment is not harmful, and further to show that it has the desired effect. In particular, health economists are concerned with maximising efficiency, i.e. maximising benefit for a fixed cost, or minimising cost for a given benefit. There are two aspects to measuring benefit: quality and quantity of life. A treatment is beneficial if it reduces morbidity and therefore increases a person's quality of life; or if it saves their life, and increases their length of life.

There are many different ways of measuring benefit: in monetary terms, life years saved or descriptions of improvements. The savings in future medical expenses from an immunisation programme could be measured in monetary terms. Saving of lives can be measured in physical terms as the number of life years saved. However, some savings can only be measured descriptively, such as subjective measures of the reduction in pain. Ideally, it would be simplest to reduce all costs and benefits to monetary terms, and hence be able to compare directly across treatments and disease groups. However, this is not possible as monetary values cannot easily be attached to reductions in pain, and would be highly subjective.

To allow an adjustment to be made for the different starting points, benefit should always measure a change. This means taking a measurement before and after an intervention, and looking at the change in health status. The health status level after the intervention alone is inadequate, as this will depend as much on the starting level as on the intervention itself. Benefit is often measured using questionnaires. Frequently, patients measure their own outcomes pre, during and post treatment. These latter results may then be compared to the pre-treatment baseline.

Having established why it is important to measure benefit, this chapter now focuses on the different ways it can be measured. Measurements may concentrate on a narrow aspect of health or take broad dimensions of a person's well-being. There are several types of measurement; these range from clinical measurement, to disease-specific measurement to generic-based measurement to preference-based measurement. Clinical measurement focuses on a very specific component of health such as blood pressure. Disease-specific and generic measures can be very broad and multidimensional. It is the focus of each type of measure that differs. Disease-specific measures are designed to capture information about one particular disease, and are thus designed around the well-known problems people face, for example, with arthritis. Generic measures try to capture all aspects of a person's quality of life. They can be used across disease groups. Preference-based measures are derived from choices, either observed or from surveys and questions to the general public, specific groups or an individual.

Firstly, different types of health measurement are discussed in this chapter, and well-validated examples of each type are included. Next, preference-based measures used to elicit valuations for health states from first principles are considered. Finally, commonly used instruments that depend on preference-based techniques for measuring health status are discussed.

Clinical measurement

Clinical measures pinpoint a specific aspect of health accurately – for example, cholesterol measured by levels of low-density lipoprotein (LDL) or high-density lipoprotein (HDL). A clinical measure can be used to determine whether a successful outcome is achieved or not. In terms of a cholesterol-lowering drug or statin being administered to a patient, a successful outcome can be deemed to have been achieved if a high-risk patient reaches the National Cholesterol Education Program Panel guideline of 100 mg/dl per patient.[1] Similarly the change in the score may be the variable of interest. A 1% decrease in LDL-C has been equated to a reduction in risk of coronary heart disease of 2–3%.[2] A cost per percentage decrease of LDL-C could then be calculated. Other measures may include X-rays or test results, blood pressure, and degree of movement, grip strength or red blood cell counts.

Disease-specific measures

Disease-specific measures investigate symptoms and effects of a particular disease directly. Although particular to one disease, their focus can be very broad. They have thus been designed to be sensitive to small, but clinically significant, changes in health status. Using disease-specific measures should avoid asking irrelevant questions. However, disease-specific measures may be too narrowly focused to include all aspects of a person's health. It is therefore usual to use a broader measure alongside them. For example, if a drug is very effective at treating arthritis, a disease-specific measure would pick up on the reduction in pain and greater mobility, yet might miss significant side effects caused by the drug.

A couple of disease-specific measures will now be considered from different disease groups, namely osteoarthritis and cancer. These provide examples of different scales and scoring methods, and show the variations in the breadth of function covered by different measures.

Western Ontario and McMaster Universities Osteoarthritis Index (WOMAC)

The WOMAC[3,4] is a three-dimensional health status measure evaluating pain, stiffness and physical function in subjects with osteoarthritis of the knee or hip. It is self-administered and takes less than five minutes to complete. It is sensitive enough to detect small but clinically significant changes in health status. Two forms are available, one on a Likert scale, the other on a visual analogue scale (VAS). The Likert scale allows subjects to respond on a five-point scale from 0 ('none') to 4 ('extreme'). The VAS allows subjects to respond anywhere on a 10 cm line marked 'none' at the left-hand end, and 'extreme' at the right-hand end.

Scoring is straightforward. For each dimension on the Likert scale, the score is the sum of the assigned values of the appropriate questions. Five questions evaluate pain, so the range of scores for pain is 0–20. Two questions evaluate stiffness, so the subscale score has a range of 0–8. Physical function has a range of 0–68, since there are 17 questions. On the VAS, the length from the left-hand side is measured in millimetres to calculate individual question scores. Scores for the individual components are summed to give three subscale scores. The range of scores is thus 0–500 for pain, 0–200 for stiffness and 0–1700 for physical function. The WOMAC can be seen in use in Angst *et al.* (2002).[5]

Functional Assessment of Cancer Therapy (FACT)

The FACT is part of a larger set of quality of life questionnaires known as the Functional Assessment of Chronic Illness Therapy (FACIT) questionnaires. These are a collection of self-reporting measures designed for those with cancer or other chronic conditions. The FACT questionnaires began with a core questionnaire known as Functional Assessment of Cancer Therapy – General (FACT-G).[6,7] This can be used for patients with any form of cancer. Now in its fourth version, FACT-G covers four main areas: physical, social, emotional and functional well-being. It comprises 27 items, each with a five-point scale. The FACT-G can be self-reported in five minutes. English versions are available free of charge, once permission has been obtained from the developer, David Cella. It is available in many different languages. The FACT-G is a widely used assessment tool for adult cancer patients in North America.

FACT questionnaires are designed to supplement the FACT-G for specific types of cancer, treatment or symptoms. The FACT-L is for patients with lung cancer and includes relevant questions regarding shortness of breath and chest pain. The FACT-Br is a supplementary questionnaire for patients with a brain tumour and includes questions about concentration and memory. Treatment-specific scales exist (for example, for those undergoing bone marrow transplants) and symptom-specific scales exist for those with fatigue. The FACT-G can be seen in use in Meyers *et al.* (2004).[8]

Disease-specific measures can be used in cost effectiveness studies to measure the effect of treatment and subsequent economic effects of competing treatments in a single disease area. Information on other disease-specific measures can be found in Bowling (2001).[9]

Generic measurement

Generic measures try to capture a person's all-round health-related quality of life, encompassing their physical, mental and social health. Their general nature allows comparisons to be made across disease groups. This is an important feature as it allows them to be used in allocative decision processes across disease states.

Generic measures of health can encompass a range of different assessment tools ranging from a simple one-dimensional question, such as whether you are feeling 'worse' or 'better' post treatment, to more complex measurement. More complex generic measures can take the form of profile measurement on the one hand, or Quality Adjusted Life Year (QALY) measures on the other. In profile measurement the multiple dimensions of health are considered separately. In QALY measurement the multiple dimensions of a person's health are collapsed into a single common index measure of health for either a single health state, or across multiple states and time periods such as in the Healthy Year Equivalent (HYE).

Since generic measures are so broad, they tend not to be sensitive enough to detect small changes in one specific aspect of a particular condition. Therefore it is usual to include a disease-specific measure to capture the symptoms specific to a condition. This section will examine profile measures, QALYs and HYEs.

Profile measures

Profile measures are broad measures of health status, and provide a profile of scores for the different dimensions of health including usual activities, mobility, sleep and emotional state. One of the most common profile measures is the Short-Form 36 and this is described in more detail below.

Short-Form 36 (SF-36) and other Short-Form versions

The SF-36[10] is a well-used and validated health status measure, which originates from the RAND Corporation's Medical Outcomes Study (MOS). The 36 questions cover eight dimensions:

- physical functioning
- social functioning
- role limitations due to physical problems
- role limitations due to emotional problems
- mental health
- energy and vitality
- pain
- general health perception.

Item scores for each dimension are summed and transformed to an ordinal scale between 0 and 100, poor health to good health. There is one further question asking the subject about their perceived change in health over the last 12 months. The eight dimensions of the SF-36 can be collapsed into two dimensions: the physical and mental component scores.[11] The SF-36 can be seen in use in Ostör *et al.* (2005).[12]

The 36 questions take five to ten minutes to complete. It is recommended for people aged 14 and over. The SF-36 has been used successfully in postal surveys except among the elderly. For this group, the SF-12 (described below) may be easier to complete and therefore more appropriate.

There is a UK version of the SF-36, where some of the language has been anglicised, and a small change has been made to the coding of one of the social functioning items. The UK version and scoring details can be purchased from the Department of Public Health and Primary Care, University of Oxford.

The standard (chronic) version of the SF-36 is most commonly used, and asks patients to report on their health state over the last four weeks. There is, however, an acute version, which asks patients to report on the last week.

Version 2 of the SF-36 was introduced in 1996. Slight changes have been made to the layout and the wording of a couple of questions. Most significantly, the questions relating to the two role-functioning dimensions now have five-choice response scales, instead of the two choices they had previously. More information on version 2 in the UK can be found from Ware (2000)[13] and Jenkinson *et al.* (1999).[14]

Other Short-Forms are available. The SF-12 has just 12 questions, and provides physical and mental component scores.[15] Although derived from the SF-36, the SF-12 does not have the same depth and scope. In version 2 of the SF-12, it is possible to produce scores for the full eight dimensions, although further work is required to establish their validity. However, when just the two summary measures are required, the SF-12 has been shown to produce virtually identical scores to the SF-36, with greatly reduced patient burden.[16]

The SF-8 is a newer and even briefer Short-Form. It is designed to replace both the SF-36 and the SF-12. Eight questions provide eight dimensions, as well as the two summary component scores. However, the SF-8 is in its early stages, and has been used very little to date. This form is available for the standard four-week recall, the acute one-week recall and also for a 24-hour recall period.

The SF-36 is at present difficult to use in an economic evaluation, because the scoring system does not produce a single, overall measure. The scoring method is not based on preferences and assumes equal intervals between scores, and also that all items are equally important. However, work is in progress to map the SF-36 to a preference-based measure of health, enabling a single index to be derived that could be used in economic evaluations. John Brazier[17,18] has led work to reduce the SF-36 to the six-dimensional SF-6D health state classification; then undertaken a survey of the general population to value a sample of health states; and finally identified a model suitable for predicting values for all health states defined by the reduced SF-36. Considerable research is required in this area: the SF-6D is still in its early stages.

Further information on all the Short-Forms can be found at http://www.sf-36.org. Information on licensing can be found at http://www.qualitymetric.com/products/descriptions/sflicenses.shtml (or by following links from the above website). The SF-36 has been translated into numerous languages, and information on the available languages for each of the Short-Forms is available with the licensing information.

Quality Adjusted Life Years (QALYs)

Preference-based measures (discussed later) for deriving utility values for health status can be used to produce a Quality Adjusted Life Year. Utility scores are combined with quantity of life to form the QALY. It allows length of life and quality of life to be combined in a single measure.

The value of each health state, usually expressed as being between 0 (dead) and 1 (perfect health), is multiplied by the number of years spent in that state. This produces the QALY. If a person lives in a health state valued at 0.7 for 10 years, this represents $0.7 \times 10 = 7$ QALYs. Therefore 10 years of health state value 0.7 is equivalent to seven years of life in perfect health (valued at 1.0). The QALY plays a significant role in health economic analysis. The QALY values may then be combined with cost to determine the cost utility for healthcare options. The QALY can be used to compare healthcare programmes since costs and benefits can be combined in a common index – cost per QALY. This is a useful tool since it can be used across patient groups. A number of validated instruments to collect QALYs exist.

Healthy Year Equivalents (HYEs)

Healthy Year Equivalents are an alternative to QALYs. HYEs assess a lifetime health profile of a series of health states rather than individual health states. HYEs are defined as the number of years in full health that are equivalent to a lifetime health profile. There is a practical problem with using HYEs. It is labour intensive, since it is necessary to estimate the number of HYEs for every health profile. Although QALYs are more common, HYEs are used widely in North America. Further discussion of the merits and problems of QALYs and HYEs can be found in Johannesson *et al.* (1996).[19] This also reviews methods for constructing both measures.

Clearly there is little point using a broad generic measure if it is unlikely to detect a small, yet clinically significant difference.

However, care must be taken with clinical measures in particular and disease-specific measures, which may not take into account the full effect of the treatment, or allow comparisons to be made across patient groups. For example, it would be misleading to conclude that a drug should be recommended because it reduces blood pressure effectively, if that same drug is found to have unpleasant side effects. It is important to consider the whole picture. In practice, patients often complete a battery of questionnaires, with generic and disease-specific or clinical measures included.

The type of measure used dictates the subsequent economic evaluation technique that may be used. Use of a single clinical measure of benefit is necessary for cost effectiveness analysis and to determine technical efficiency (*see* Chapter 1). It is capable of measuring differences between two or more different treatments in the same clinical area; similarly disease-specific indicators may be used in this way. Cost utility analysis by contrast seeks to determine not only technical but also allocative efficiency (*see* Chapter 1). It allows comparison across different disease areas and requires the use of preference or index-based outcome measures.

Preference-based measures

Measures based on preferences that provide a single index are of most interest to health economists. Only these measures can be used in cost utility analysis. Preferences are derived from choice, often from the general public. A number of different techniques are used for eliciting preferences from individuals. These are discussed first and then a number of different instruments that are underpinned by such techniques are presented.

A number of different methods can be used for eliciting preferences for health status. The most widely used methods for eliciting individuals' valuations of health states are visual analogue scales, magnitude estimation, standard gamble, time trade-off and person trade-off, and a further method is willingness to pay. These are described below.

Visual analogue scale (VAS)

The visual analogue scale is a straight line on which respondents are asked to mark on their valuation of a health state. The VAS is also known as the rating scale, direct assessment, and category scaling.

The line may be horizontal or vertical, and is often 10 or 20 cm long. End points will usually be clearly marked, although in some cases, respondents are asked to mark on the worst and best possible health states. Although VAS scoring is a simple method to use, it requires professional printing to ensure that the line is accurate in length. The EuroQol Thermometer is an example of a VAS. (The EuroQol is discussed later in this chapter.)

The simplest way to ascertain a person's preferences for a group of health states is to ask them to rank them from least preferred to most preferred, and then to place the health states on a scale, so that the intervals between them represent the difference in preference. A VAS can be used to measure an individual's before and after treatment pain scores, for example, by marking their pain levels on the VAS before and after treatment.

As well as placing the health states on the VAS, respondents may be asked to mark on it the worst and best possible health states. The interval from worst to best possible health state is transformed to be from 0 to 1. It is the intervals between health states on the line rather than the actual values given that are of most interest.

This is an easy method to use. However, many health economists question its theoretical validity, as respondents are not asked to make choices. Scarcity has led economic theory to be built on choices and opportunity costs of forgoing one item for another. This method is not built on such theory.

It is reasonable to believe that the VAS can be used to rank health states. However, it is questionable whether a change from 0.3 to 0.4 is the same as from 0.8 to 0.9, and hence whether the VAS is truly an interval scale and differences between the ranks are meaningful.

Magnitude estimation (ME)

Magnitude estimation asks respondents to estimate the magnitude of the difference between two health states. Respondents may value health state A as being three times better than health state B. This is therefore a ratio scale. A set of health states can be valued if sufficient questions are asked. By measuring the relative values between each of the health states a meaningful or cardinal measurement is achieved. If, for example, state A is twice as good as state B and state B twice as good as state C, it will follow that state A is four times better than state C.

Standard gamble (SG)

The standard gamble approach to eliciting preferences asks subjects to choose between an uncertain outcome of perfect health but with the risk of death and a definite outcome in a health state less than perfect health. Individuals are offered two options. Alternative 1 has two possible outcomes: a probability p of perfect health for x years and a probability of 1-p of immediate death. Alternative 2 is a definite outcome of a particular state *i*, which is less than perfect health (poor vision, for example) for x years. The probability p is varied until the subject is indifferent between the two alternatives. This is the utility for state *i*, where 0 is immediate death, and perfect health is 1. These choices are shown in Figure 7.1. Since it is difficult to relate to probabilities, visual aids are often used to assist subjects. A probability wheel, consisting of a disc with two coloured sectors that can be turned around to adjust the amount of each colour showing, can be used to represent the probabilities p and 1-p.

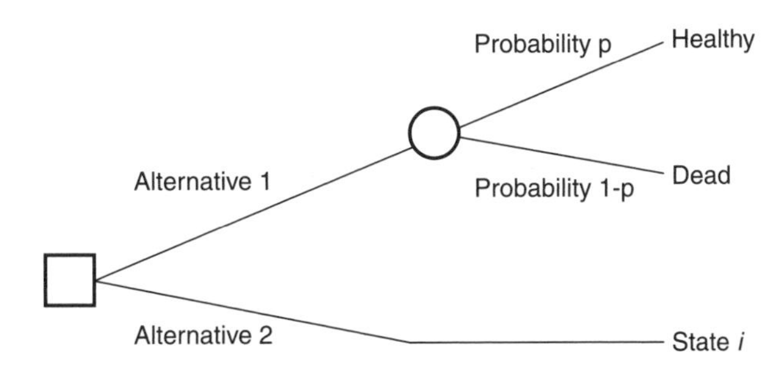

Figure 7.1 The standard gamble method.

For example, one may rate the need for tooth caps at 0.99 – that is, a person is only prepared to take a 1% risk of dying to have tooth capping undertaken – whereas the need for a hip replacement (i.e. a state of chronic disability and pain) may result in a rating of 0.5 – that is, one would accept a 50% risk of death as the indifference point of remaining in the state permanently.

Time trade-off (TTO)

The time trade-off method asks subjects to choose between shorter periods of healthy life, and longer periods of life in poorer health. Health and longevity are traded off until individuals are indifferent between them. Individuals are offered two options. Alternative 1 is t years of life at health state h_i, followed by death. Alternative 2 is x years of life (x < t) in a state of perfect health (a state better than h_i), followed by death. The time x is varied until subjects are indifferent between the two alternatives. The utility score of the health state *i* is then x/t. This method is shown in Figure 7.2. So if a subject is indifferent between ten years with arthritis, and eight years of perfect health, then the quality weight is 0.8.

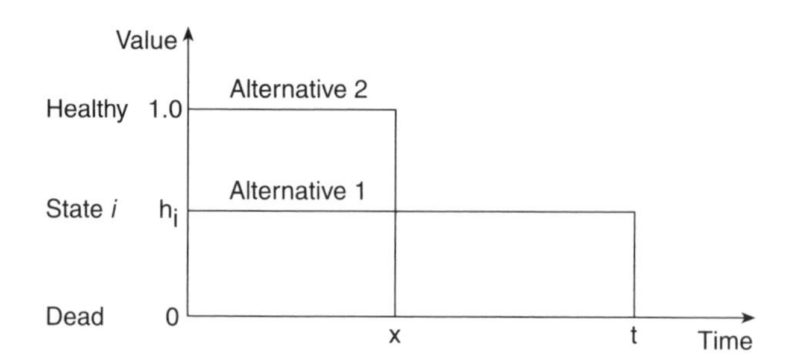

Figure 7.2 The time trade-off method.

The principle used in TTO is that of trading survival for increased quality of life. A good example of the TTO exercise used in practice is in eye disease.[20] Eighty consecutive patients with macular degeneration and a vision of 20/40 from an eye clinic in Philadelphia were asked to complete a TTO exercise. Respondents were asked to place a value on quality of life in five different vision-defined groups ranging from perfect vision to a number of legally blind states. The average remaining life expectancy for the group was 12.1 years. The group members were willing to give up 3.2 years of life in return for perfect vision, thus giving a mean quality of life value for macular degeneration of (12.1 – 3.2)/12.1 or 0.72. The exercise further demonstrated that different visually impaired states produce different quality of life values depending upon the severity of the state. Individual group values for quality of life ranged from 0.89 for perfect vision to 0.4 for only being able to perceive light.

Person trade-off (PTO)

The person trade-off method asks subjects to decide how many people with a condition x would need to have their lives extended by one year for that to be equivalent to an extra year's life for 100 healthy people. A different way of phrasing the question would be to compare two groups of ill people, one with disease x and one with disease y. Each group contains a different number of people. The respondent is asked to choose between treating the group with disease x or disease y. The numbers in the groups are varied until the respondent is indifferent between the groups. The value of the health state is given by x/y (the numbers in each group). Making decisions in this way is a way of expressing collective social choice rather than being based on individual decision making and consumer sovereignty. It can be argued such decisions are intuitively appealing and more meaningful to decision makers.[21] PTO is a relatively new technique and the evidence on reliability and theoretical validity is still underdeveloped.

Willingness to pay (WTP)

Willingness to pay enables a monetary value to be placed on an event or treatment option. It a useful technique for determining an individual's preferences for treatment or to avert a negative outcome, where no market value readily exists. Individuals are asked for the maximum amount they are willing to pay to gain a treatment or avert an event. This may be, for example, to gain access to a new surgical technique. One problem with the technique is whether people's answers to a hypothetical question truly reflect real behaviour. A variation on the technique is to look at people's revealed preferences – that is, their behaviour in similar real-life situations (for example, paying for car safety features or lifestyle decisions) – and draw inferences to health accordingly.

Deriving health-state valuations from first principles should give a fair and true reflection of how a population values a health state. It is not though a costless exercise. Not only do people struggle with making choices about hypothetical situations, but they may not totally understand the probability values presented to them in such exercises. Deriving such values from first principles is very time consuming, and requires dedicated research time to administer such exercises to participants.

Instruments used to measure health status

Instruments used in cost utility analysis are discussed below. They include the EuroQol, the Quality of Well-Being Scale, the Health Utilities Index and the Disability Adjusted Life Year. The measures depend upon preference-based techniques in their derivation.

EuroQol (EQ-5D)

Designed by the EuroQol Group,[22,23] the EQ-5D is a short but effective health status measure. The EuroQol health status measure is commonly used to provide quality weights for use in QALYs. It has five dimensions:

- mobility
- self-care
- usual activities
- pain and discomfort
- anxiety and depression.

Each dimension is a section on the EQ-5D questionnaire, and each has three statements ranging from 'no problem' to 'some problems' to 'unable to do'. For each dimension, respondents are asked to tick one statement that best describes their health state that day. Responses to these questions are usually given as a five-digit descriptor. For example, a subject whose responses are 11223 has no problems with mobility or self-care, moderate problems with usual activities and pain, and extreme problems of anxiety or depression.

There are 245 different health states, including death and being unconscious. Each of these health states can be converted to a score, which has been derived from data collected from a survey of approximately 3000 of the general public in the UK.[24] The time trade-off method was employed to elicit these preferences; this method was discussed earlier in this chapter. Scores are on a cardinal scale. They range from 0 (representing death) to 1 (representing perfect health). A few scores are less than zero, indicating that it is possible to be in a state worse than death; the worst health state is valued at −0.59.

There is also a visual analogue scale for subjects to rate their own health. This is a vertical line marked 0 (worst imaginable health state) at the bottom and 100 (best imaginable health state) at the top.

The EQ-5D is appropriate for a wide range of conditions, and provides a single index that can be used both in a clinical and economic evaluation.

An example of the EuroQol in practice can be seen in Table 7.1. This is adapted from James *et al.* (1996) [25] and shows the health status valuations, cost and cost per QALY (EQ-5D) following elective orthopaedic surgery. The table presents a summary of the results ranked in order of greatest benefit for patient valuations. The first column shows the health state valuation obtained from the patients' assessment of their health status before and after surgery and projected over their lifespan. Similarly, the second column is the consultants' perceived assessment of the individual patients' improvement in health status. Cost remains constant whether patient or consultant health status valuations are used and is taken from patient-based costing. The final two columns represent cost divided by QALY (patient and consultant respectively), which places costs and QALYs in a common unit and shows for each procedure how much must be spent to gain an additional QALY per person. Hence the lower the figure in these two final columns, the more cost effective the procedure.

Table 7.1 QALYs (EQ-5D) and costs in elective orthopaedic surgery

Operation	**Net health gain EQ-5D**		**Cost (£)**	**Cost (£) per QALY (EQ-5D)**	
	Patient valuations	**Consultant valuations**		**Patient**	**Consultant**
Spinal discectomy	6.830	12.831	2044	299	159
Primary hip ≥40 y	6.270	9.351	3112	496	333
Primary hip < 40 y	6.108	3.759	3546	580	943
Primary knee	2.955	5.880	4134	1 399	703
Carpal tunnel	1.309	4.050	132	101	33
Dupuytren's	1.262	0.000	708	561	N/A
Flexor tenosynovectomy	0.190	1.847	2032	10 672	1100

Primary hips <40 y and ≥40 y are those patients aged under 40 years and 40 years or above respectively.
N/A = not applicable.
Source: Adapted from James *et al.* (1996), Table 5.[25]

The actual priority listing or ranking is similar between patients and doctors; however, it can be seen that the magnitude of benefit perceived is different in the two groups. Doctors in this sample often rated health gain as higher than the patients' valuations for the same procedures. The greatest health gain is from spinal discectomy, hip replacement and knee surgery. The most cost effective procedure in term of cost per QALY is carpal tunnel, generating a QALY for only £101.

More information on the EQ-5D can be found at http://www.euroqol.org. The EQ-5D has been translated into numerous languages: there are 60 official language versions, with others awaiting official approval (January 2005).

Quality of Well-Being Scale (QWB)

The Quality of Well-Being Scale[26] was one of the first measures designed to combine length and quality of life in a single index. It is used to assess two aspects of a person's health: their functional status and current symptoms. It has been found necessary to use an interview format rather than relying on self-administration, in order to obtain the complete picture. The first part of the interview measures functional status in terms of three dimensions: mobility, physical and social activities. The second part of the interview aims to identify symptoms present in individuals over the previous six days. There are 26 symptoms included, as well as death (which is not on the interviewee's card). Where more than one symptom is found to be present, the most undesirable is scored.

Preference weights have been obtained for each function level. Overall QWB scores range from 0 (death) to 1 (complete well-being), although scores less than 0 representing states worse than death do also exist. Each dimension level (below the highest) has an associated negative weight. The weights for the three functional dimensions and the symptoms are subtracted from 1 to calculate a person's score.

The focus of this questionnaire is principally on physical problems, with few items specifically covering emotional states. Despite this, scores do correlate well with other measures of mental well-being, indicating that physical and mental problems affect each other, and hence covering one aspect covers the other. The QWB has been criticised for its scoring methods, where some disabled states are valued as being better than less disabled states.

The major criticism of the QWB was the need for the interview format, which made it more expensive and difficult to administer than other tools. In response to this, a self-administered version known as the Quality of Well-Being Self-Administered Scale (QWB-SA) was developed.[27] The QWB-SA asks respondents to report symptoms over the last three rather than six days. The checklist of symptoms has been expanded, and there is a greater emphasis on items that assess mental health.

The QWB-SA was used to assess treatments for preventing diabetes in a paper by the Diabetes Prevention Program Research Group.[28] The health utilities scores were then used to calculate QALYs gained by treatment groups.

The QWB can be used with any type of disease. It has been used in osteoarthritis and rheumatoid arthritis, as well as AIDS and cystic fibrosis. Information on obtaining the instrument can be found at http://www.outcomes-trust.org.

Health Utilities Index (HUI)

The Health Utilities Index is a further example of a multi-attribute scale. It is a North American based measure. There are three HUI systems: HUI1, HUI2 and HUI3. All are preference-based interval scales and are a progression from each other in their content. Like the EQ-5D they have 0 as dead and 1 as perfect health and have some states valued negatively (that is, worse than death). They all use preference values from members of the public to derive the scores. A time trade-off approach was used to value health states in the original HUI1. The original HUI[29] classification system was based on the QWB.

The HUI1, now superseded by HUI2 and HUI3, contained four attributes: physical function (including mobility and physical activity), role function (including self-care), social–emotional function (including emotional well-being and social activity), and health problem. It was originally developed to measure neonatal intensive care outcomes and is hence unique in the multi-attribute scales listed as it has its origins in child health rather than adult health.

The HUI2[30] built on the HUI1 and was expanded in order that it could be used in measuring outcomes from children in general. It was initially used to measure outcomes in childhood cancer. Six attributes formed the core of the HUI2 system: sensory and communications ability (comprising vision, hearing and speech); happiness; self-care ability; pain or discomfort; learning and school ability; and physical activity ability. An additional category of fertility was added; this was disease-specific to childhood cancer. This additional category could be dropped when using the HUI2 in diseases other than cancer. Values for the health states were obtained using a sample of parents of schoolchildren and applying a standard gamble technique.

Both the HUI2 and then the HUI3 were subsequently modified for adult applications. The fertility term was dropped and the sensory and communications ability attribute was split into three separate attributes: vision, hearing and speech. This enabled structural independence of all the attributes to be achieved. A random sample of adults was used to obtain the health state values for HUI3, again using the standard gamble technique. The standard 0 to 1 scale was used with some states being valued as worse than death.

All the HUI classifications require the answers given by respondents to be translated into the corresponding health state valuations. HUI2 and HUI3 can be completed in about ten minutes by means of a simple self-administered questionnaire. Self-administered questionnaires have advantages both in anonymity and time when conducting research that requires outcomes measurement. HUI2 and HUI3 can be seen in use in Barr *et al.* (1999).[31] The questionnaire is available in a number of languages. Further information on the HUI can be found at http://www.fhs.mcmaster.ca/hug.

Disability Adjusted Life Years (DALYs)

The Disability Adjusted Life Year[32] is a further example of a utility measure in healthcare. It was developed by the World Health Organization (*see* Chapter 6). Unlike the QALY, it measures health loss averted rather than health gain. DALYs are measured on a scale of 0 to 1, where 0 represents no problems, and 1 represents death or a health state equivalent to death.

The original DALYs were based on a classification of six illness states and weights derived from a group of experts. The new adjusted DALYs use a person trade-off approach to derive the utility weights attached to disability states. They were originally developed in the field of public health to determine the global burden of disease. If, for example, the number of DALYs lost from diarrhoea is 10.4 DALYs per 1000 population in sub-Saharan Africa and from cancer is 1.5; these figures would suggest targeting resources to diarrhoea. This, however, says nothing about the cost effectiveness of the interventions.

The DALY has been used to represent a measure of cost effectiveness, with results presented in terms of cost per DALY saved. The numbers of papers that have been published using a

DALY as a measure of cost effectiveness are limited, with the majority based on studies undertaken in developing countries.[33]

The measures presented above are examples of well-validated, commonly used, preference-based measures. These are all utility-based measures, which are particularly useful for economic evaluations because they enable cost utility analysis to be performed.

Conclusion

There are many ways in which benefits can be measured for healthcare purposes. There is no gold standard approach that can be recommended. The most appropriate method to use will depend on the nature of the benefit measurable, and the purpose for measuring it. Different measures of benefit ranging from the clinical measures to utility-based measures will serve different types of economic analysis, from cost effectiveness analysis to cost utility analysis. Benefit measurement is a vital part of the remit of a health economist.

References

1 National Cholesterol Education Program (2002) *Third Report of the National Cholesterol Education Program (NCEP) Expert Panel on Detection, Evaluation and Treatment of High Blood Cholesterol in Adults (Adult Treatment Panel III)*. National Institutes of Health Publication No. 02-5215. Also available at http://www.nhlbi.nih.gov/guidelines/cholesterol/atp3full.pdf.
2 Law MR, Wald NJ and Thompson SG (1994) By how much and how quickly does reduction in serum cholesterol concentration lower risk of ischaemic heart disease? *BMJ*. **308**: 367–72.
3 Bellamy N, Buchanan WW, Goldsmith CH *et al.* (1988) Validation study of WOMAC: a health status instrument for measuring clinically important patient relevant outcomes to antirheumatic drug therapy in patients with osteoarthritis of the hip or knee. *Journal of Rheumatology*. **15**(12): 1833–40.
4 McConnell S, Kolopack P and Davis AM (2001) The Western Ontario and McMaster Universities Osteoarthritis Index (WOMAC): a review of its utility and measurement properties. *Arthritis and Rheumatism*. **45**(5): 453–61.
5 Angst F, Aeschlimann A, Michel BA *et al.* (2002) Minimal clinically important rehabilitation effects in patients with osteoarthritis of the lower extremities. *Journal of Rheumatology*. **29**(1): 131–8.

6 Cella DF, Tulsky DS, Gray G *et al.* (1993) The Functional Assessment of Cancer Therapy scale: development and validation of the general measure. *Journal of Clinical Oncology*. **11**(3): 570–9.
7 Brucker PS, Yost K, Cashy J *et al.* (2005) General population and cancer patient norms for the Functional Assessment of Cancer Therapy – General (FACT-G). *Evaluation and the Health Professions*. **28**(2): 192–211.
8 Meyers FJ, Linder J, Beckett L *et al.* (2004) Simultaneous care: a model approach to the perceived conflict between investigational therapy and palliative care. *Journal of Pain and Symptom Management*. **28**(6): 548–56.
9 Bowling A (2001) *Measuring Disease: a review of disease-specific quality of life measurement scales* (2e). Open University Press, Buckingham.
10 Ware JE and Sherbourne CD (1992) The MOS 36-Item Short-Form Health Survey (SF-36). I: Conceptual framework and item selection. *Medical Care*. **30**(6): 473–83.
11 Jenkinson C (1998) The SF-36 physical and mental health summary measures: an example of how to interpret scores. *Journal of Health Services Research and Policy*. **3**(2): 92–6.
12 Ostör AJ, Richards CA, Prevost AT *et al.* (2005) Diagnosis and relation to general health of shoulder disorders presenting to primary care. *Rheumatology*. **44**(6): 800–5.
13 Ware JE (2000) SF-36 Health survey update. *Spine*. **25**(24): 3130–9.
14 Jenkinson C, Stewart-Brown S, Petersen S *et al.* (1999) Assessment of the SF-36 version 2 in the United Kingdom. *Journal of Epidemiology and Community Health*. **53**: 46–50.
15 Jenkinson C and Layte R (1997) Development and testing of the SF-12. *Journal of Health Services Research and Policy*. **2**(1): 14–18.
16 Jenkinson C, Layte R, Jenkinson D *et al.* (1997) A shorter form health survey: can the SF-12 replicate results from the SF-36 in longitudinal studies? *Journal of Public Health Medicine*. **19**(2): 179–86.
17 Brazier J, Usherwood T, Harper R *et al.* (1998) Deriving a preference-based single index from the UK SF-36 Health Survey. *Journal of Clinical Epidemiology*. **51**(11): 1115–28.
18 Brazier J, Roberts J and Deverill M (2002) The estimation of a preference-based measure of health from the SF-36. *Journal of Health Economics*. **21**: 271–92.
19 Johannesson M, Jonsson B and Karlsson G (1996) Outcome measurement in economic evaluation. *Health Economics*. **5**: 279–96.
20 Brown GC, Sharma S, Brown MM *et al.* (2000) Utility values and age-related macular degeneration. *Archives of Ophthalmology*. **118**: 47–51.
21 Richardson J (1994) Cost-utility analysis – what should be measured? *Social Science and Medicine*. **39**: 7–21.

22 The EuroQoL Group (1990) EuroQoL – a new facility for the measurement of health-related quality of life. *Health Policy*. **16**(3): 199–208.
23 Rabin R and de Charro F (2001) EQ-5D: a measure of health status from the EuroQol Group. *Annals of Medicine*. **33**: 337–43.
24 Dolan P, Gudex C, Kind P *et al.* (1996) The time trade-off method: results from a general population study. *Health Economics*. **5**: 141–54.
25 James M, St Leger S and Rowsell KV (1996) Prioritising elective care: a cost utility analysis of orthopaedics in the north west of England. *Journal of Epidemiology and Community Health*. **50**: 182–9.
26 Kaplan RM and Anderson JP (1988) A general health policy model: update and applications. *Health Services Research*. **23**(2): 203–35.
27 Frosch DL, Kaplan RM, Ganiats TG *et al.* (2004) Validity of self-administered quality of well-being scale in musculoskeletal disease. *Arthritis and Rheumatism*. **51**(1): 28–33.
28 The Diabetes Prevention Program Research Group (2003) Within-trial cost-effectiveness of lifestyle intervention or metformin for the primary prevention of type 2 diabetes. *Diabetes Care*. **26**(9): 2518–23.
29 Torrance G, Boyle MH and Horwood SP (1982) Application of multi-attribute theory to measure social preferences for health states. *Operations Research*. **30**: 1043–9.
30 Feeny D, Furlong W, Barr RD *et al.* (1992) A comprehensive multi-attribute system for classifying the health status of survivors of childhood cancer. *Journal of Clinical Oncology*. **10**(6): 923–8.
31 Barr RD, Simpson T, Whitton A *et al.* (1999) Health-related quality of life in survivors of tumours of the central nervous system in childhood – a preference-based approach to measurement in a cross-sectional study. *European Journal of Cancer*. **35**(2): 248–255.
32 Murray CJ and Lopez AD (1994) Quantifying disability: data, methods and results. *Bulletin of the World Health Organization*. **72**(3): 481–94.
33 Fox-Rushby JA (2002) *Disability Adjusted Life Years (DALYs) for Decision Making? An overview of the literature*. Office of Health Economics, London.

8 Resources and costs

Introduction

The nature and level of detail of cost information collected in a study depends on a number of factors. These may include the resources available for the study itself; the importance of the individual cost variables in the decision-making process; and the presence or absence of other readily available data sources from which to inform cost.

The previous chapters in this book have concentrated upon obtaining such information from secondary sources and in an aggregated format. This chapter will address how to obtain such information for yourself, from first principles.

A detailed micro-costing exercise, often referred to as bottom-up costing or an ingredients approach, is where the resource data are collected from first principles in a study. The resource use is quantified directly rather than relying upon secondary sources of data. This is the most detailed and potentially accurate route by which to quantify resources.

The approach requires that certain key areas must be addressed and processes be in place for the exercise to work, for example that a suitable data collection form be available for use with the patient or health professional. Similarly, a route for administering the form must be available whether directly at a clinic, by telephone or through the post. Adequate personnel need to be available and willing to collect such data, in the form of dedicated researchers or existing professionals who may undertake the role as part of the wider clinical research process. There must be a clear understanding of the data required and the reason for their collection. These issues will be discussed in detail in the rest of this chapter.

The design and conduct of such an exercise are likely to need the assistance of a professional health economist. Input from a well-informed research partner – for example, the managerial decision maker, the medical consultant, pharmacist, research nurse or physiotherapist – will enhance the nature and level of detail collected and helps ensure its relevance. An understanding of this area is therefore of importance to a health professional.

Economics is concerned with the actual measurement of the natural resource units required to perform a service or intervention, such as the number of doctors required in surgery and the type and number of drugs used – this is rather than the cost or monetary value *per se*. It is the actual number of units of resource employed that will represent the true value of the activity. Once the actual resources employed have been identified, the appropriate costs can be attached to the natural units, whether these be local costs or national costs, to obtain the actual valued cost of the service or intervention. Hence:

$$\text{units of resource} \times \text{unit cost of resource} = \text{actual cost}.$$

Disaggregating resources and costs in this manner enables the decision maker or analyst to see the true picture and adapt other work to their own local situation.

If such an approach can be pursued it will yield significant advantages, yet it is not without its problems. These will be discussed below.

Advantages of micro costing

Collecting data by individually designed proformas on dedicated resource use allows a high level of detail to be obtained on the actual resources consumed in an intervention, which is often masked when using aggregate or national figures. It may be, for example, that an intervention has an effect on length of stay on a hospital ward. The broad-level data may suggest a five-day length of stay. The cost of each of these days (if using national Reference Costs, for example) will be valued the same, e.g. at £200 per day. Collecting the data in a bottom-up fashion may reveal a more interesting and useful picture. The five days may, for example, comprise an initial two days which are highly resource intensive both in staff time and consumables, whereas the final three days may really only comprise hotel costs. Any changes in ward staffing levels or consumables that failed to reflect this would overcompensate for the length of stay effect. Increasing the staff intensity for all five days would be unnecessary. This helps to illustrate the difference between the average and the marginal cost. Hence the greater level of detail in the costs improves the accuracy of such figures.

Collection of appropriate resource data may help not only to inform the study in question, but better inform future studies. If the work undertaken showed that drugs have little effect on the overall cost whereas staff time is a large and important input, future research can give less weight to the collection of drug information and may wish to establish an even greater level of detail on staff time. It could go from a simple recording of time allocated to an intervention, to a more sophisticated apportionment of staff time to the period of the day.

Disadvantages of micro costing

The approach proposed is labour intensive, time consuming and hence costly in terms of the staff time required to undertake the exercise. Exact identification of all the possible variables, and the method and nature in which to collect them, can be a complex and time-consuming process. It will require special health economic or research methodology expertise, combined with an in-depth knowledge of the actual process of the intervention in order to ensure that no key component of data collection is missed. The process of the intervention itself may span a number of healthcare areas ranging from secondary care to primary care with different professional groups involved, so hence may need to employ the skills of a large number of professionals to execute the bottom-up approach.

Completion of the bottom-up approach will require access to both the patients and their records. This may be difficult to achieve. Consent will be required for both types of contact. The records may be stored in a number of different areas and in different formats; it is then costly to synthesise each of the individual components together and hence to analyse the data, both in terms of time and technical complexities. Patient contact can be difficult to achieve. To contact the patient in the healthcare centre – either hospital or primary care – the researcher must coordinate a number of tasks and conflicting demands on both theirs and the patient's time for this to be achieved. Once the patient has left the healthcare environment and returned home, further contact can be even more difficult.

The data collection instrument

Bottom-up costing means that considerable effort will have to be made to collect the costs that are actually incurred in an intervention and its alternatives using primary sources. Gathering such resource information requires considerable thought to be given to the nature of the variables for which this information is required. The analyst must put considerable thought into deciding which variables to collect and in what natural units the resources will be measured.

The first task is therefore to identify the key variables for which detailed information is required. It may be that detailed information on a few variables will be adequate rather than having to collect information on all the resources utilised during an intervention. Identification of the key resource variables can be guided by recourse to the literature, i.e. quantifying those variables that other researchers have identified as the major cost drivers. Similarly expert opinion can be used to inform this process.

An alternative approach is to collect data on all the variables in the study in order to identify as full a cost picture as possible. Whether all or a few variables are to be included in the exercise, a data collection form will be required to obtain the information.

What costs will you measure?

Costs can be split into direct and indirect costs. These are described next.

Direct costs

Direct costs are those that occur directly because of an intervention. Costs can be collected in a number of different areas. A useful distinction in the collection of cost information is staff, capital and consumables. Again, when deciding upon whether one or all of these areas will be measured in detail, it is important to keep a focus upon the likely key cost drivers. The following sections detail the three main categories of direct cost.

Staff

Certain interventions may be highly resource intensive of staff time, while other treatment choices may involve direct comparison between a very labour-intensive treatment (for example, physiotherapy) and a pharmaceutical intervention. It is important to quantify accurately the staff and their time into these interventions to differentiate truly between the alternatives, and thus ensure that the interventions are compared fairly with no hidden costs ignored.

It is not always possible from broad-level data to assign truly the nature of the staff performing the intervention either in terms of time or grade. A bottom-up costing approach therefore attempts to identify the grade of staff that performs the intervention and to allocate the time spent on each activity. It may be important in terms of the research question to break up the time into direct patient contact and indirect patient contact, related activities and administrative duties. Counting the exact minutes of time spent on each activity can be difficult. Often, therefore, time is apportioned in terms of defined units (for example, 15 minutes, half an hour) or more broadly to a slot such as a morning or an afternoon.

Capital

All the capital equipment, whether buildings or machines (technology), used in an intervention should be identified. The present cost of capital must then be calculated. This depends upon the cost of the capital and the expected length of life of the capital equipment. These two figures along with the discount rate (or annuity) can be used to calculate the annual capital cost for the equipment. This would assume that the whole of the capital is employed for the whole time on the intervention – this may not be the case. A further apportionment may be required. Such apportionment will depend on the actual time attributable to the intervention. This apportionment must take into account whether the equipment can be used by someone else. If not, even if the equipment is not fully employed – that is, used for 100% of the time for the intervention – the total capital cost must be apportioned to that intervention.

Consumables

Whether data on the consumables required for an intervention are to be collected by the patient, healthcare worker or a researcher, the method for collecting them and the exact nature and units in which they are to be collected should be clear and simple to all concerned. At the simplest level this requires specifying the unit for collection, whether that be, for example, a drug name and dose or simply listing a test performed. Secondly, the number and frequency requires recording – was it, for example, two packs, three tablets for 30 days, etc.? This should be consistent across the consumable categories. All drugs should be recorded by intervention route, e.g. oral or injection, by dose/tablet per day and the number of days for the regime recorded.

Table 8.1 illustrates an example of a form that could be used to collect drug costs.

Indirect costs

Table 8.1 Example record of all drugs and therapies administered to patient

Medication/therapy	Total daily dose	Unit	Route*	Duration (in days, weeks, etc.)
1 e.g. cimetidine (400 mg)	800	2	1	2 weeks
2				
3				
4				
5				
6				
7				
8				

* Route: 1 = oral, 2 = subcutaneous, 3 = intramuscular, 4 = intravenous.

Indirect costs are concerned with the financial consequences that occur because of an intervention – that is, they are incurred because of an intervention but are not directly attributable to the intervention. It may be important not only to measure the direct cost of an intervention but to measure the indirect costs.

The most important variable associated with indirect cost is that of productivity, and the effect on an individual in terms of gains and losses in productivity or employment because of an intervention. In practice the hypothesis may be: does the individual lose time from paid employment because of an illness or intervention, or do they return to work quicker with one intervention over another? The measurement of indirect cost is therefore important where the intervention choices have differential effects on return to work.

Increasingly studies are called upon to consider the indirect cost effects of an intervention. An example of such a choice is in terms of open or laproscopic surgery for gallstones. Although the laproscopic surgery is more technologically intensive it yields a shorter recovery time for the patient and hence a quicker return to work.

Determining the value of an individual's productivity poses a number of challenges. Unless the average wage rate is imputed it is necessary to elicit some way of imputing the individual's actual wage rate. Asking direct questions to a respondent regarding their salary is often considered to be a sensitive area. A way of eliciting a value for a person's employment without directly asking for their salary is to ask them for their occupation. An average salary can then be imputed for that occupation. The question may indeed be even broader than occupation and may just broadly follow the OPCS social class classification of professional, managerial, skilled manual, semi-skilled, and manual. Again it is then left to the analyst to impute an average wage rate for each of the salary bands. Obviously this is not a wholly accurate measure of the indirect costs but a second-best scenario for calculating the indirect costs.

Two further categories that require careful handling are those of the housewife and the unemployed. It has been suggested that the wage rate for unemployed is taken to be 25% of the average wage rate or the cost of leisure.[1] The wage for a housewife may be imputed as a shadow price or taken from a near market – that is, a market with similar attributes and tasks performed. The component parts of a housewife's role may be broken down and defined as cooking, cleaning, etc., and the salary for each of these tasks may be taken from those who are paid, for example, to cook and clean. Using this information therefore and examining near markets, the value of a housewife may be in the region of £13 000 per annum.[2]

Collecting resource and cost information

Resources and costs can be collected from a number of sources: health records and information systems, staff and the patient themselves.

The patient

Information regarding resources can be elicited directly from the patient. Whether this is to be completed independently by the patient themselves or recorded with the help of the health professional or researcher, the key message is to keep this information clear and simple.

Ideally the patient should not be asked to provide information regarding events longer than three months after the event took place. There is evidence to suggest that patient memory is unreliable after a three-month period and declines in a linear fashion between three and 12 months.[3] Memory is further affected by type of event and patient group. The recall of, for example, a surgical episode in a 45 year old four months after the event may be more accurate than whether a course of tablets was taken four months ago by a 90 year old.

Structured information is often the most useful for an economic evaluation although other social scientists would argue that this is too restrictive and argue for a more open-ended approach to the collection of information. Patient diaries are one such approach; these are often unstructured and require the patient to keep a record, on a daily basis, of key events and resources. They may, for example, be semi-structured and ask about nutritional intake or whether the patient visited a GP or hospital during a defined period. A big problem with such an approach is the patient's incentive to complete this record on a daily basis. The information may not be entered at all or entered some time after the event took place. Unstructured diaries are even more difficult to analyse and to elicit information.

Alternatively the patient can be given a detailed and structured sheet to fill in regarding their use of health service resources over a defined period. This may be sent out in the post with a return prepaid envelope provided to the patient for completion, or may be administered during a regular follow-up appointment. Postal surveys may be poorly completed with the patient having little incentive to return the questionnaire. Completion may be improved by a follow-up reminder telephone call.

An expert group was convened in the mid-1990s to develop a comprehensive patient costing questionnaire. The results of their work are reported in a working paper.[4] The group's aim was to review all the existing measures for collecting patient information both on direct and indirect costs and to bring them together in a comprehensive patient costing questionnaire. The questionnaire was designed to be used on a section-by-section basis and to enable information to be collected both in considerable detail and in a more truncated form depending on the study objective.

The hospital

Secondary care data can be collected on a number of items, mainly staff, capital and consumables as already discussed. This section will concentrate on the key data that may be collected from the hospital sector.

One of the problems for the researcher or analyst is that many data are already collected within the hospital sector. The data may be stored, however, in a number of different places from a number of different sources and for a number of different reasons. The information contained within each of the individual systems may be inadequate to address the analytical or research question; for example, the hospital information system will record length of stay but this may be only one part of the information required by the researcher. Data collection tools are therefore used not only to record events from first principles or when they happen, but to pull together and extract information from a number of different sources and existing systems.

The data collection tools therefore may contain a section on length of stay (obtainable from the hospital information system); on drugs used (from the pharmacy system); and on biochemical and blood tests (from the pathology system). It can therefore be a tool to direct the analyst towards what information to collect and towards the existing information systems that may contain such information.

The same data collection tool may of course be used to collect the information directly, by either the health professional (e.g. the nurse or the doctor completing the information) or from the patient themselves.

Other information that may be important to collect in secondary care is individual contacts with key professionals – for example, doctors, nurses, physiotherapists and dieticians. This may be extended to include professionals not directly within the secondary care environment such as social workers or Macmillan nurses. Similarly, it may be important to collect information on certain aids and appliances used in treatment.

Secondary care information not only relates to the inpatient stay but includes all outpatient appointments and attendances including, for example, day case wards. Again, a similar amount of detail may be required on the outpatient visit (for example, the tests performed, the staff attending, etc.). Outpatient information systems have been historically less well developed than inpatient systems.

The primary care centre

Information systems in primary care are less well developed than in secondary care. Hence, it may be even more important to collect information from first principles in primary care, as existing individual or practice data may not exist. The slow uptake of computerised records and data collection systems in primary care and the ɩparate geographical spread of primary care practices make obtaining this information more difficult.

The information collected in primary care may include frequency and duration of visit; location of visit (for example, home or surgery); and health professional (for example, GP, district nurse, community physiotherapist or health visitor). It may further include clinical data such as drugs prescribed and their duration, tests, diagnosis and concomitant conditions.

The degree of computerisation can influence how easy it is to collect information. Computerised information may only reveal a partial picture – it may not, for example, accurately indicate consultation time. Some practices may have been computerised for a long time so may easily be able to retrieve retrospective information; others may have only recently become computerised. Data on computer records may not be complete or there may be a time lag between an event and data entry. The hospital consultant's letter, for example, may not immediately be entered onto the system.

Information may be collected from either the patient themselves, the GP or the practice manager. It is imperative that in all cases any information retrieval form is easily understood by all and is easy to complete. The patient may either fill the form in at a practice visit, or more likely be asked to complete such information retrospectively in the form of a postal survey. If medical staff are to complete such information from records, unless it is directly completed during a consultation it would be preferable if clerical or administrative staff could complete the necessary information. GP time is the most expensive staff component within community care, and time spent completing forms is an opportunity cost in terms of direct patient contact time.

When should you collect resource and cost information?

Resources and costs data may either be collected prospectively (for example, as part of a randomised controlled trial) or retrospectively through audit once an intervention has been implemented.

Prospective data collection

Collection of data prospectively has the advantage that the information is seen as integral to the study. Collecting the information immediately helps to overcome the problems of patient and professional recall after an event. It minimises the potential for missing data when trying to collect data from secondary sources retrospectively. It can be quicker in terms of research time to collect data when the event happens through the addition of a couple of extra data collection pages, compared with trying to track the data down across primary and secondary care sources once the event has happened – for example, having to find the original case records, find the relevant page and then extract the relevant information.

Collecting such data prospectively can add an additional data collection burden to a study. This burden may be deemed to be too great or expensive to be implemented alongside the study. It may be felt that increasing the information required prospectively may jeopardise the whole information retrieval system, in that patients or professionals may vote with their feet and fail to complete any information for the study.

Retrospective data collection

Collecting data retrospectively reduces the actual burden placed upon a randomised controlled trial. Retrospective data collection may give the researcher chance to collect information at a more convenient time rather than within the time pressures of the study itself.

Finding the information retrospectively can be cumbersome and time consuming. Data may be missing and impossible to retrieve or recreate retrospectively. Queries regarding the data can be difficult to clarify after the event.

Conclusion

This chapter has examined the issues surrounding collecting data from first principles – the advantages and disadvantages. It has suggested why this may be necessary, what sort of data may be collected and which sources may be utilised to collect the data. It has discussed the qualities and possible content of a good data collection instrument. Further it has examined issues around the timing of such data collection. Collecting data from first principles is not something to be undertaken lightly; however, it can reap many rewards in terms of the level and nature of information such an exercise yields.

References

1 Mackie PJ, Wardman M, Fowkes A *et al.* (2003) *Value of Travel Time Savings in the UK: Summary Report to the Department of Transport.* http://www.dft.gov.uk/stellent/groups/dft_econappr/documents/pdf/dft_econappr_pdf_610340.pdf.

2 Department for Works and Pensions (2005) *Labour Force Survey (LFS) Historical Quarterly Supplement. Table 36: Average gross weekly/hourly earnings by occupation.* http://www.nationalstatistics.gov.uk/STATBASE/Expodata/Spreadsheets/D7936.xls.

3 Evans C and Crawford B (1999) Patient self-reports in pharmacoeconomic studies. Their use and impact on study validity. *Pharmacoeconomics.* **15**(3): 241–56.

4 UK Working Party on Patient Costs (2001) *An Annotated Cost Questionnaire for Completion by Patients.* HERU Discussion Paper No. 03/01. University of Aberdeen, Aberdeen. 92 pages.

9 Reflections and futures

Introduction

Healthcare and its technology are an ever-evolving world. Planning and delivering such healthcare require tools and techniques that assist in managing this changing and challenging environment. In addition it is important to have an understanding of the structure and outputs of the healthcare system. The population has grown and aged over the last 50 years. At the same time the number of new technologies is increasing and continuing to add to the armoury from which to fight disease. This is set against a population who have greater expectations of healthcare than previous generations. Not only do they wish to see their life expectancy increase compared to their predecessors, but they expect life to be at a better quality for longer. The challenge for those who manage healthcare is to provide more quantity and more quality from a wider range of treatment options, but still within a budget of limited resources – hence choice and scarcity, as introduced at the beginning of this book.

Health economics as both a discipline and a profession has grown in the last 50 years. It has been driven by the need to better prioritise the healthcare provided. This book has taken the reader through the techniques of health economics and its role in achieving efficiency under conditions of scarcity.

The growth and application of sources of economic data

With the requirement to manage healthcare resources more effectively, new organisations have been established to provide such healthcare. Existing organisations have had new and changing roles in managing healthcare. With the formation and evolution of the organisations empowered to provide healthcare, the collection and sophistication of the routine data have improved significantly during this period. The growth of such data has enabled the items required for economic analysis to become more readily available. At the same time it has created pressures to collect specifically economic data – for example, to inform NICE decisions on the funding of new technologies.

The book has examined the analytical techniques available to the health economist and their meanings, and then addressed practically the types of data and information available in healthcare at a national, secondary and primary care level. This has been considered in terms of its usefulness in health economic decision making and its application. The rich wealth of information to support health economic decision making would have been incomplete without considering the organisations in the sphere of healthcare and the economically useful data they provide. In the last sections of the book, healthcare benefits and resources are considered separately. The complex and diverse issues surrounding benefit measurements are discussed. Finally, the development of individual datasets and data required in terms of the resource elements of healthcare are examined.

Applied health economics seeks to address real-world questions and answer them with recourse to the inputs and outputs of different options or the costs and the benefits of healthcare. What is clear is that health economics and information to support health economic decision making is not an area that sits in isolation from the rest of healthcare or indeed public policy and decision making. Information is produced for many reasons and not necessarily for health economists or health economic decision making or analysis, but such diverse information can be used to help answer health economic questions and achieve economic objectives such as efficiency. An initial problem for decision makers is to begin to comprehend the vast wealth of information routinely available and to be able to access this information quickly and painlessly. The challenge is to both understand and use the available data in order to aid health economic decision making.

It is unlikely any single source can answer an economic question. Part of the role of the analyst or decision maker is to utilise the required, appropriate and available data to assist in the process. Equally, it is unlikely that there will be a single combination of data and information sources that must be used to answer a question. A number of differing sources may be used to answer the same question. Again the challenge is to decide on the right sources at the right time that fit the decision maker's personal situation.

This book has focused on using and interpreting existing data and information sources in order to address issues from the perspective of health economics. It has attempted to provide a comprehensive review of the available sources and their uses; it is then left to the individual analysts to decide which source is right for them. The book has suggested ways in which to supplement the existing data where appropriate using actual data on costs and benefits. The information contained within this text should assist in this process.

The book has shown that there are many competing demands on healthcare resources. It has demonstrated that achieving economic outcomes such as efficiency can benefit the whole population by maximising the potential benefits from scarce resources.

Target audience

All those who work and study in the healthcare field have a responsibility to manage and use such resources to the best of their ability in order that society maximises the amount of healthcare, and ultimately health, available to the population. Health economics can help in this process. By this token health economics is everyone's responsibility and appropriately using the resources available, whether in terms of the staff or drugs or the available information, is important.

The book is aimed at anyone who is involved with the delivery or commissioning of healthcare. It examines the problem of optimal allocation of scarce resources in healthcare for those who are involved in delivering and managing such care, from the nurse at the ward level to the manager at the national level. It looks at practical data sources and the nature and function of the information that they provide. This is set within the practical application of the health economist's toolkit in order to achieve efficiency within healthcare – that is, maximum benefit from a given resource.

Similarly, it is an important asset for anyone who is involved with studying health and healthcare in order that they may get a better understanding of the issues and problems and possible solutions to the allocation of a scarce resource – healthcare. The book should be helpful for students of health economics or health services research at the postgraduate level. It introduces the reader to basic health economic concepts and how to apply them to their specific contexts. As a text it should further be of use to those academics already in the field both as a teaching aid and as a comprehensive resource for the latest sources of information available from which to inform an economic appraisal.

What health economics has to offer

Health economics is concerned with both the real resources and costs employed to deliver healthcare and the outcomes or benefits that they produce. This has then been examined in the interrelationship between costs and benefits and efficiency – that is, maximising the benefit per unit of resource.

Scarcity is the bottom line in healthcare, as there will always be more competing wants than there will be resources available to deliver all that is desired of a healthcare system. It is important for a decision maker or analyst to be able to utilise all the information and tools available to them. This is so that they can determine the opportunity cost – that is, the costs and benefits to their organisation, or to society or to the individual – of pursuing one particular healthcare decision over another. It is important therefore that they can critically appraise such costs and benefits. This will require access to analytical methods that will equip them with the tools, such as cost effectiveness and cost utility, that will enable them to process such information in a comprehensive and useable form.

Levels of health economic information

What is clear is that economic data and information that can help inform decision making and analysis exist at many different levels and in many different guises. Many of these data sources are interrelated. Primary and secondary care data inform national data, and national data have an important role to play in the planning of primary and secondary care services. Similarly, some data may only be readily available at a national aggregate average level whereas other sources of economic information are accessible at a hospital trust or practice level. Similarly primary, secondary and national decision makers may access the same information sets and sources. What will have become clear is that there is no single set of data or information source that must be used to solve a health economic problem or answer a health economic question. There are many possible ways in healthcare to answer a question surrounding the use and outcomes of healthcare resources. The health service is data rich – it is knowing what data exist and how to use and access this wealth of data and information that is important.

The text has taken the reader through the types of information available at each level and more importantly how to use and interpret such information in terms of health economic analysis. The coverage and depth of data are encouraging, ranging from the national casemix measures and Reference Costs, down to each hospital trust's individual waiting list statistics. Further, it is important not to ignore the availability of locally produced data and databases. In contrast to this there are the agreements around pharmaceutical pricing that take place at a national level to determine a nationally recognised set of costs for drugs. The key is that data and information to assist health economic decision making are available at many levels and from many sources and cover a broad spectrum of healthcare costs and benefits.

It is important to be aware which organisations can provide useful information in terms of health economics. It may be easier for a decision maker to be regularly updated of the information provided by a particular organisation, or to target such an organisation in the first search for data rather than trying to locate a specific item of technical information in its own right. It is important to note that it is not only healthcare organisations that provide information that is useful for analysis and decision making, but related organisations such as academic institutions, economic bodies and social care organisations. Further it must be recognised that useful information is not in the domain of the public sector alone. Often it is the mix between the public and private sector in healthcare that is important. This is especially true when thinking of the data provided for and by the pharmaceutical industry.

The application of clear health economic thinking is not merely about using and accessing data. It is necessary, as we have shown throughout the text, to understand the underlying thinking behind the components of the economic problem, and similarly in the resources that input into healthcare costs. Discussion of health economic information for decision making would be incomplete without understanding more fully the meaning of these two areas.

Health benefit, as we have shown, is dependent on the viewpoint chosen and can comprise strictly clinical and disease-based measures through to more functional forms of health benefit and the ability to perform the activities of daily life. Importantly in health economics it includes the preference or utility-based measures of health benefit that are so important when combined with the resource-level information to give a measure of efficiency. Again we can see that the level of health benefit data chosen will govern whether we are able to answer questions surrounding technical efficiency in health-care or allocative efficiency. A whole wealth of literature exists in the measurement of benefit alone. This text seeks to inform the reader of the many facets of benefit measurement, point them in the direction of obtaining such information, and help them to gather such information themselves should they so wish.

Much of this text has been devoted to finding sources for measuring and valuing resources in healthcare. Again it is imperative that as a healthcare analyst or decision maker what constitutes a resource and as such a healthcare cost is clearly understood. It is real resources that matter in healthcare: buildings and equipment (capital); doctors and managers (staff); bandages and drugs (consumables); and the resources that are incurred by patients and society including indirect resource use such as time off work. Knowing and understanding the resource structure for a healthcare intervention is crucial for understanding the cost structure. It may then be used to determine what the key cost drivers are in any intervention and on whom the costs of an intervention fall.

It is the interrelationship between both costs and benefits that differentiates health economic evaluation from purely clinical or management decision making. Although both sides of the equation are important, to determine the efficiency gain to primary care, the hospital, the nation or the patient, costs and benefits cannot be considered in isolation. It is the relationship between costs and benefits that matters. This book has provided the reader with the means to determine both the costs and benefits of healthcare interventions. It has further provided the tools that enable both costs and benefits to be related and as such the determination of the most efficient allocation of healthcare resources.

The text has demonstrated that health economic decisions occur at many different stages in healthcare. Choices exist at many different levels in the delivery and consumption of healthcare. They may exist around whether to deliver more elderly care, or increase the nation's capacity to undertake screening programmes. Choices must be made, for example, over whether to use simvastatin or rosuvastatin in the primary care drug treatment of cholesterol; or over whether to increase the amount of physiotherapy care for shoulder pain or use GPs to give a steroidal injection. All of these are important and real choices in healthcare. The challenge for health economics is to equip the decision maker with some of the tools to enable them to address this multiplicity of competing choices and diverse areas to do the *best* for their target population.

The future

The data and information required for health economic decision making constitute an ever-evolving area. The need for good economic decision making will not diminish as healthcare expectations and innovations increase, but will continue ever more to be necessary to ensure that the population gets the best out of the resources available for healthcare. We have seen that health economic data and information exist at many different levels in healthcare, from primary care to the national level, and the decisions that such data inform in health economic terms are made at each and every level in healthcare from the hospital ward to parliament. It is hoped that this textbook has gone some way to assist its readers in making such decisions and in unravelling some of the mysteries surrounding the information required for such decision making.

Index